Since the
Prague Spring

Since the Prague Spring

The Continuing Struggle for Human Rights in Czechoslovakia

Edited by HANS-PETER RIESE

Translated from the German by Eugen Loebl

Vintage Books
A Division of Random House
New York

Library of Congress Cataloging in Publication Data

Main entry under title:

Since the Prague spring.

   Translation of Bürgerinitiative für die
Menschenrechte
   Includes index.
   1. Civil rights—Czechoslovakia. I. Riese,
Hans-Peter. II. Title.
Law   342'.437'085   78-51410
ISBN 0-394-72556-5

VINTAGE BOOKS EDITION, January 1979
FIRST EDITION

Manufactured in the United States of America

Foreword by Arthur Miller

1   BASIC POLITICAL DOCUMENTS

A Ten-Point Declaration on the First Anniversary
of the Occupation   *3*

An Excerpt from the Final Act of the Helsinki Conference on Security and Cooperation in Europe   *9*

Charter '77   *11*

2   LETTERS TO GUSTÁV HUSÁK, PRESIDENT AND SEC-
RETARY GENERAL OF THE CENTRAL COMMITTEE OF
THE COMMUNIST PARTY OF CZECHOSLOVAKIA

Introduction by Hans-Peter Riese   *17*

Milan Hübl to Gustáv Husák   *19*

Václav Havel to Gustáv Husák   *23*

An Appeal by Relatives of Political Prisoners   *40*

3   LETTERS AND APPEALS TO VARIOUS POLITICAL IN-
STITUTIONS AND LEADERS

Introduction by Hans-Peter Riese   *47*

To the Czechoslovak Citizenry   *50*

Dr. František Janouch to the Chief Justice of the Supreme Court   *52*

Pavel Kohout to Dr. Milan Klusák, Minister of Culture of the Czechoslovak Socialist Republic   *54*

Alexander Dubček to the Federal Parliament of Czechoslovakia and the Slovak National Council   *64*

Dr. František Kriegel, Dr. Gertruda Sekaninová-Čakrtová, and František Vodsloň to the Federal Parliament of Czechoslovakia   *86*

Karel Kaplan to the Leadership of the Communist Party and of the Government of Czechoslovakia   *91*

4   LETTERS AND DECLARATIONS TO FOREIGNERS

Introduction by Hans-Peter Riese   *97*

Karel Kosík to Jean-Paul Sartre   *100*

Jean-Paul Sartre to Karel Kosík   *104*

Pavel Kohout to Heinrich Böll and Arthur Miller   *106*

Ludvík Vaculík to Kurt Waldheim, Secretary General of the United Nations   *113*

Vilém Prečan to the Participants of the World Congress of Historians in San Francisco, August, 1975   *121*

Anna Šabatová to all Communist and Workers' Parties   *129*

Zdeněk Mlynář to the Communists and Socialists of Europe   *135*

An Open Letter from Various Czechoslovak Writers to Heinrich Böll   *146*

Heinrich Böll to Jaroslav Seifert   *149*

Pavel Kohout: His Own Position   151

Appendix   155
Editor's Afterword   202
Biographical Notes   204

Foreword

It is always necessary to ask how old a writer is who is reporting his impressions of a social phenomenon. Like the varying depths of a lens, the mind bends the light passing through it quite differently according to its age. When I first experienced Prague in the late sixties, the Russians had only just entered with their armies; writers (almost all of them self-proclaimed Marxists if not Party members) were still unsure of their fate under the new occupation, and when some thirty or forty of them gathered in the office of Liszty to "interview" me, I could smell the apprehension among them. And indeed, many would soon be fleeing abroad, some would be jailed, and others would never again be permitted to publish in their native language. Incredibly, that was almost a decade ago.

But since the first major blow to the equanimity of my mind was the victory of Nazism, first in Germany and later in the rest of Europe, the images I have of repression are inevitably cast in Fascist forms. In those times the Communist was always the tortured victim, and the Red Army stood as the hope of man, the deliverer. So to put it quite simply, although correctly I think, the occupation of Czechoslovakia was the physical proof that Marxism was but one more self-delusionary attempt to avoid facing the real nature of power, the primitive corruption by power of those who possess it. In a word, Marxism has turned out to be a form of sentimentalism toward human nature, and this has its funny side. After all, it was initially a probe into the most painful wounds of the capitalist presumptions; it was scientific and analytical. What the Russians have done in Czechoslovakia is, in effect, to prove in a Western cultural environment that what they have called socialism simply cannot tolerate even the most nominal independent scrutiny, let alone an opposition. The critical intelligence itself is not to be borne, and in the birthplace of Kafka and the absurd in its subtlest expression, absurdity emanates from the Russian occupation like some sort of gas which makes one laugh and cry at the same time.

Shortly after returning home from my first visit to Prague mentioned above, I happened to meet a Soviet political scientist at a high-level conference where he was a participant representing his country, and I was invited to speak at one session to present my views of the impediments to better cultural relations between the two nations. Still depressed by my Czech experience, I naturally brought up the invasion of the country as a likely cause for American distrust of the Soviets, as well as the United States aggression in Vietnam from the same détente viewpoint.

That had been in the morning; in the evening at a party for all the conference participants, half of them Americans, I found myself facing this above-mentioned Soviet whose anger was unconcealed. "It is amazing," he said, "that you—especially you as a Jew—should attack our action in Czechoslovakia."

Normally quite alert to almost any reverberations of the Jewish presence in the political life of our time, I found myself in a state of unaccustomed and total confusion at this remark, and I asked the man to explain the connection. "But obviously," he said, (and his face had gone quite red and he was quite furious now) "we have gone in there to protect them from the West German Fascists."

I admit that I was struck dumb. Imagine!—the marching of all the Warsaw Pact armies in order to protect the few Jews left in Czechoslovakia. It is rare that one really comes face to face with such fantasy so profoundly believed by a person of intelligence. In the face of this kind of expression all culture seems to crack and collapse; there is no longer a frame of reference.

In fact, the closest thing to it that I could recall were my not infrequent arguments with intelligent supporters or apologists for our Vietnamese invasion. But at this point the analogy ends, for it was always possible during the Vietnam war for Americans opposed to it to make their views heard, and, indeed, it was the widespread opposition to the war which finally made it impossible for President Johnson to continue in office. It certainly was not a simple matter to oppose the war in any significant way, and the civilian casualties of protest were by no means few, and some—like the students at the Kent State College protest—paid with their lives. But what one might call the unofficial underground reality, the version of morals and national interest held by those not in power, was ultimately expressed and able to prevail sufficiently to alter high policy. Even so, it was the longest war ever fought by Americans.

Any discussion of the American rationales regarding Vietnam must finally confront something which is uncongenial to both Marxist and anti-Marxist viewpoints, and it is the inevitable pressure by those holding political power to distort and falsify the structures of reality. The Marxist, by philosophical conviction, and the bourgeois American politician by practical witness, both believe at bottom that reality is quite simply the arena into which determined men can enter and reshape just about every kind of relationship in it. The conception of an objective reality which is the summing up of all historical circumstances, as well as the idea of human beings as containers or vessels by which that historical experience defends itself and expresses itself through common sense and unconscious drives, are notions which at best are merely temporary nuisances, incidental obstructions to the wished-for remodeling of human nature and the improvements of society which power exists in order to set in place.

The sin of Power is to not only distort reality but to convince people that the false is true, and that what is happening and quite clearly happening is only an invention of enemies. Obviously, the Soviets and their friends in Czechoslovakia are by no means the only ones guilty of this sin, but in other places, especially in the West, it is possible yet for witnesses to reality to come forth and testify to the truth. In Czechoslovakia the whole field is preempted by the Power itself.

Thus a great many people outside, and among them a great many artists, have felt a deep connection with Czechoslovakia—but precisely because there has been a fear in the West over many generations that the simple right to reply to Power is a tenuous thing and is always on the verge of being snipped like a nerve. I have myself sat at dinner with a Czech writer and his family in his own home and looked out and seen police sitting in their cars down below, in effect warning my friend that our "meeting" was being observed. I have seen reports in Czech newspapers that a certain writer had emigrated to the West and was no longer willing to live in his own country, when the very same man was sitting across a living-room coffee table from me. And I have also been lied about in America by both private and public liars, by the press and the government, but a road—sometimes merely a narrow path, always remained open before my mind, the belief that I might sensibly attempt to influence people to see what was real and so at least to resist the victory of untruth.

I know what it is to be denied the right of travel outside my country, having been denied my passport for five years by our Department of State. And I know a little about the inviting temptation to simply get out at any cost, to quit my country in disgust and disillusion, as no small number of people did in the McCarthy fifties, and as a long line of Czechs and Slovaks have in these recent years. I also know the empty feeling in the belly at the prospect of trying to learn another nation's secret language, its gestures and body communications without which a writer is only half-seeing and half-hearing. More important, I know the conflict between recognizing the indifference of the people and finally conceding that the salt has indeed lost its savor and that the only sensible attitude toward any people is cynicism.

So that those who have chosen to remain as writers on their native soil despite remorseless pressure to emigrate are, perhaps no less than their oppressors, rather strange and anachronistic figures in this time. After all, it is by no means a heroic epoch now; we in the West as well as in the East understand perfectly well that the political and military spheres—where "heroics" were called for in the past—are now merely expressions of the unmerciful industrial-technological base. As for the very notion of patriotism, it falters before the perfectly obvious interdependence of the nations, as well as the universal prospect of mass obliteration by the atom bomb, the instrument which has doomed us, so to speak, to this lengthy peace between the Great Powers. That a group of intellectuals should persist in creating a national literature on their own ground is out of tune with our adaptational proficiency that has flowed from these developments. It is hard anymore to remember whether one is living in Rome or New York, London or Strasbourg, so homogenized has Western life become. The persistence of these people may be an inspiration to some but a nuisance to others, and not only inside the oppressing apparatus but in the West as well. For these so-called dissidents are apparently upholding values at a time when the first order of business would seem to be the accretion of capital for technological investment. It needs hardly be said that by no means everybody in the West is in favor of human rights, and Western support for Eastern dissidents has more hypocritical self-satisfaction in it than one wants to think too much about. Nevertheless, if one has learned anything at all in the past forty or so years, it is that to struggle for these rights (and without them the accretion of capital is simply the construction of a more modern prison) one has to struggle for them wherever the need arises.

That this struggle *also* has to take place in socialist systems suggests to me that the fundamental procedure which is creating violations of these rights transcends social systems—a thought anathema to Marxists but possibly true nevertheless. What may be in place now is precisely a need to erect a new capital structure, be it in Latin America or the Far East or underdeveloped parts of Europe, and just as in the nineteenth century in America and England it is a process which always breeds injustice and the flaunting of human spiritual demands because it essentially is the sweating of increasing amounts of production and wealth from a labor force surrounded, in effect, by police.

The complaining or reforming voice in that era was not exactly encouraged in the United States or England; by corrupting the press and buying whole legislatures, capitalists effectively controlled their opposition, and the struggle of the trade-union movement was often waged against firing rifles.

There is of course a difference now, many differences. At least they are supposed to be differences, particularly that the armed force is in the hands of a state calling itself socialist and progressive and scientific, no less pridefully than the nineteenth-century capitalists boasted of their Christian ideology and their devotion to the human dimension of political life as announced by the American Bill of Rights and the French Revolution. But the real difference now is the incomparably deeper and more widespread conviction that man's fate is *not* "realistically" that of the regimented slave. It may be that despite everything, and totally unannounced and unheralded, a healthy skepticism toward the powerful has at last become second nature to the great mass of people almost everywhere. It may be that history, now, is on the side of those who hopelessly hope and cling to their native ground to claim it for their language and ideals.

The oddest request I ever heard in Czechoslovakia, or anywhere else, was to do what I could to help writers publish their works—but not in French, German or English, the normal desire of sequestered writers cut off from the outside. No, these Czech writers were desperate to see their works—in Czech! Somehow this speaks of something far more profound than "dissidence" or any political quantification. There is something like love in it, and in this sense it is a prophetic yearning and demand.

—ARTHUR MILLER

1

Basic Political Documents

A Ten-Point Declaration on the First Anniversary of the Occupation

Addressed to the Federal Parliament, the Czech National Council, the Czechoslovak Federal Government, the Czech Socialist Republic, and the Central Committee of the Communist Party

One year has passed since representatives of the government and Party were taken to Moscow and the so-called Moscow Protocol was formulated. This Protocol belittles a mature people, who have been unfortunate enough to become the pawn of two superpowers. The one that sent us its armies claimed that socialism was endangered in our country. It was not. What was at stake was the reputation of people who had preached socialism for twenty years.

The democratization of the country in 1968 convinced the people that mistakes can be corrected, that injustice can be undone, and that people can enjoy their work. At that time the government and the new Communist Party were on the way to proving that socialism is not necessarily connected with repression and economic scarcity. On the contrary, it can offer all the traditional freedoms that were fought for in previous revolutions and a blueprint for a society both economically and morally superior to any other. Our attempts were in harmony with the old ideals of the socialist movement, which since its beginnings has stood for national sovereignty and individual self-determination, and has condemned imperialism, shady diplomacy, and partisanship. It is the duty of everybody in the international socialist community not to interfere in our affairs, to treat us honorably, and to leave it to the Czechoslovak people to avoid restoring an outdated, reactionary social order.

For a whole year we have been living under conditions

imposed on us. During this time our lives have become more difficult. The economy is faltering, prices are climbing, production goes unplanned, and the causes of these crises have not been discovered. Many able and gifted elected officials have had to leave their jobs. The Action Program of the Communist Party of Czechoslovakia has been revoked in its entirety, civic organizations have been paralyzed by the government's interference, the public has been excluded from the decision-making process, and not a single organ of political power is based on the will of the people. The mandate of the Federal Parliament has expired. And censorship makes it impossible to speak openly about these matters.

This state of affairs suits old opportunists and new careerists who say whatever they like, twist facts, slander other people, organize propaganda campaigns, and who are shameless enough to tell the people that it is now possible to speak and write the truth. The fact is that one has to look for truth sideways; nobody can guarantee that information is reliable. Many have been victimized—some even imprisoned—because they tried to fulfill the functions of a free press.

We are not satisfied with these conditions and will not remain silent. We have chosen to address the legislative bodies of the republic—the Federal government, the state government, and the Central Committee of the Czechoslovak Communist Party—and have decided to make our case known, even if we risk the well-known reprisals.

1. We condemn what happened a year ago because it violates our national sovereignty and discredits socialism. We stand for the fulfillment of all international agreements. Socialist governments should show the world how misunderstandings and conflicts between them are resolved by civilized means. We regard the occupation of our country by the Soviet Army as a cause of unrest and an obstacle to the restoration of friendly relations with the Soviet Union. We demand that the highest offices of our country begin negotiations for the withdrawal of the Soviet Army.

2. We do not agree with the policy of retreat in the face of threats, which has led to the further entrenchment of the gov-

ernment bureaucracy and to purges in the state, Party, and fiscal apparatus. We protest the repression of organizations whose activities do not violate any law. We condemn the prohibition against the coordinating committee of the union of artists, and government interference in the affairs of university students.

3. We condemn censorship. It makes impossible the free exchange of thoughts and information, and the emergence of a well-informed public. It generates trashy literature, makes it difficult to check power, and encourages political immorality. It leads to a state where the arts and sciences are mere servants of the powerful.

4. We do not believe that in the future the government will respect the laws of the land and that the institutionalized crimes of the fifties will not be repeated. For those who have violated the law are not being prosecuted; they remain in key positions and are shielded from all criticism. The banning of the Society for Human Rights seems to us an evil omen.

5. We do not accept the Communist Party as a power that stands above other organizations, which are responsible to the whole nation. It is reprehensible to make Party membership a prerequisite for citizenship. We insist that the Communist Party must earn its leading role by serving the people better than any other organization. The relationship between the parties of the National Front should be balanced. Non-Communists who represent a majority should not be forced to live in conditions they have no way of influencing. We applaud those Communists who attempt to rid the party of its aberrations and who see it as their duty to realize "socialism with a human face." We support all those who insist that the legality of the XIV Party Congress held in 1968 be fully respected.

6. The occupation of our country by foreign troops has proved particularly harmful to our economy. The enactment of the law legalizing workers' councils is being postponed—and where they do exist, they are being phased out. Economic benefits are again being withheld and worker-management relations are arbitrarily established. This crisis is blamed on those who tried to put into practice economic reforms. The workers themselves are also blamed for their poor morale and low pro-

ductivity. Yet, should they work for people who should have been removed from office a year ago? Should they work harder when a higher income can't buy them what they want? We understand their mood.

Everyone needs to know that his work has meaning and must be persuaded day to day by his own experience that the leadership is acting in his own interest. Everyone should have the right to express his views regarding the economy. We believe that employees should have superiors whom they trust and respect, for it is unbearable to work for someone who is forced on you. Many of our problems can be solved by replacing incompetent bosses. Trade unions should be allowed to do so. We demand, therefore, that a law on socialist management be enacted as soon as possible. This law should guarantee that experts—while taking into consideration the state plan—will make decisions about production and that workers will have the right to participate in decisions about investments and the distribution of profit. We demand that the rights of the trade unions be fully respected according to the Charter of the Association of Trade Unions. If we speak about the class interests of the workers, we recognize that these are the interests of everyone.

8. We are glad that among the many reforms proposed by the Action Program of the CPC in 1968, at least one has been realized: the federalization of the state. We will oppose any attempt to create mistrust and conflicts between the Czech and Slovak nations.

9. Censorship makes all criticism of the government impossible. Citizens are intimidated by the state's ruthless interference in their affairs, and state organizations and dishonest newspaper editors are creating an even more frightening mood. In the face of all this we declare unequivocally that to hold a different view from that of one's government is an age-old human right. As citizens who are striving for socialist democracy and humanism, and working against everything that offends our national traditions, we exercise our right to oppose, by all legal means, all that is unreasonable. We do not intend to act outside of the law, yet we will appeal to all state organs to defend our rights. We will try to create working relationships

between national organizations. And in the same way that we deplore violence in international relations, we deplore violence as a means of solving national political problems. We will therefore demonstrate our hostility to functionaries who, under normal conditions, would have been fired a long time ago. We will do this by not seeing or listening to them, by not communicating with them in any way, and by not making use of their services. We declare our solidarity with all those who are persecuted for their political convictions.

We believe that even the most intense repression is powerless to murder thought and subvert work. Every citizen should do his work well where possible, especially if it benefits his fellow man. Scientists, intellectuals, and artists should persist in their endeavors. Young people should continue to study and learn not only what they must but also what they choose. Even in political bondage a mature nation can still successfully define its own life style and principles. Thus we may, though with some difficulty, improve housing conditions, create healthier working conditions, and fight against waste by economizing. We should cater to entertainment that is in our own taste and not accept entertainment we don't like. We should practice our hobbies. We know that the solution of our problems does not depend on us alone. We are not the center of the world and the driving force of the universe. There are times when we must simply persevere and appreciate our achievements. We are firmly convinced that progress cannot be stopped forever.

We conclude by refuting in advance all the accusations and insults we expect. We are not opportunists. We are not being hostile to the state; those who feel hurt have no right to identify themselves with the state. We only ask that the government function according to the Constitution. We are not enemies of the Party. Free discussions within the Party would prove this. Nor are we against socialism; but we are for a socialism that is proper to a highly developed country and is devoid of those repulsive features imposed upon our country by a handful of narrow-minded, dogmatic, power-hungry careerists and unscrupulous despots. We have no reason to assume an anti-Soviet attitude insofar as the Soviet Union's internal policy is concerned. We object only to brutal interference in the affairs of other nations. We wish the best of success to the Soviet people. We support the democratic forces of the whole world in their fight for international demilitarization and the peaceful solution of all conflicts.

VÁCLAV HAVEL, writer
DR. LUBOŠ KOHOUT, political scientist, university professor
VLADIMÍR NEPRAŠ, editor of the newspaper *Reporter*
LUDĚK PACHMANN, journalist
JAN TESAŘ, historian
LUDVÍK VACULÍK, writer
JAN WAGNER, deputy chairman of the Youth Council

An Excerpt from the Final Act of the Helsinki Conference on Security and Cooperation in Europe

VII. Respect for human rights and basic freedoms, including those of thought, conscience, religion, and creed

Participating nations will respect all human rights and basic freedoms, including those of thought, conscience, religion, or creed, without regard to race, sex, language, or religion.

They will promote and encourage the exercise of civil, political, economic, social, cultural, and other rights and freedoms, all of which derive from the inherent dignity of individuals and all of which are essential to their free and full development.

Participating nations will recognize and respect the rights of individuals to profess and practice, alone or with others, their religion or creed in accordance with the dictates of their own consciences.

Participating nations that include diverse minorities will respect their equality before the law and will afford them the full opportunity to enjoy all human rights and basic freedoms.

Participating nations recognize the universal significance of human rights, respect for which is essential to peace, justice, and continuing friendly relations among themselves and other countries.

They will endeavour jointly and separately, and through the United Nations, to promote universal respect for these rights.

They safeguard the right of individuals to exercise their civic duties.

Participating nations will act in accordance with the purposes and principles of the United Nations Charter and with the General Declaration on Human Rights. They will also fulfil their obligations as set forth in international declarations and agreements, including the International Agreements on Human Rights.

Helsinki, 1975

Charter '77

Law No. 120, which was passed on October 13, 1976, incorporates the International Agreement on Civil and Political Rights and the International Agreement on Economic, Social, and Cultural Rights, both of which were signed in behalf of our republic in 1968 and confirmed at the 1975 Helsinki Conference. These pacts took effect in our country on March 23, 1976. The freedoms and rights they guarantee have been the goals of progressive movements in the past, and their enaction can significantly contribute to the development of a humane society.

We welcome the fact that the Czechoslovak Socialist Republic has agreed to the Helsinki Agreements. However, their enactment is at the same time an urgent reminder that many fundamental human rights are violated in our country. For example, the right to freedom of expression guaranteed by Article 19 of the first pact is frequently infringed upon. Tens of thousands of citizens have been prevented from working in their chosen profession solely because their views deviate from the official line. They have suffered various forms of discrimination at the hands of authorities or social organizations, and have been deprived of the means to defend themselves. They are the victims of a new apartheid.

Others, numbering in the hundreds of thousands, have been deprived of the "freedom from intimidation," which the preamble of the first pact guarantees, and they live in constant fear of losing their jobs or other benefits if they express their views.

In violation of Article 13 of the second pact, which guarantees the right to education, many young people are prevented from pursuing higher studies because of their political or religious views or those of their parents. Countless others fear that if they openly state their convictions, they or their children will be deprived of an education.

The right to "seek, receive and impart information freely, regardless of whether it is oral or printed" or "conveyed through art, or any other means,"—Point 2, Article 13 of the first pact—is denied not only outside but also inside the courts, as was evidenced by the recent trial of the Plastic People of the Universe, the rock band.

Freedom of speech is suppressed by the censorship of all mass media. No political, philosophical, scientific, or artistic view deviating even slightly from the official ideology is allowed in print; public criticism of the nation's crisis is prohibited; the possibility of defending one's self against false and offensive charges made by the official propaganda machine is foreclosed, although legal protection against libel is expressly guaranteed by Article 17 of the first pact; and open discussions of intellectual and cultural matters are out of the question. Many scientists and artists as well as other citizens have been discriminated against because years ago they published or openly stated views that are now condemned by the present regime.

Religious freedom, emphatically guaranteed by Article 18 of the first pact, is systematically curbed by the limits imposed on the activities of priests, who are constantly threatened with the revocation of their licenses, and by the suppression of religious instruction in schools.

Repression in Czechoslovakia results from the subordination of all institutions and organizations of the state to the ruling party and a few highly influential individuals. Neither the Constitution of the CSSR nor the laws of the republic regulate the making of government policy. Policy makers, therefore, are responsible only to themselves; yet they exercise a decisive influence on the legislative and executive branches of the government, the judiciary, trade unions, social organizations, other political parties, businesses, institutions, and schools.

The right of assembly and the right to participate in public affairs are both denied. Workers cannot freely establish organizations to protect their economic and social interests and right to strike, as Point 1 of Article 8 of the second pact provides.

Other civil rights, stemming from the prohibition against "government interference in private life, the family, home, and correspondence," are gravely violated by the Ministry of the Interior, which controls the life of the people by tapping telephones, searching private homes, censoring the mail, hounding individuals, and relying on a network of informers. The Ministry has often interfered in the decisions of employers, encouraged discrimination, influenced the organs of justice, and supervised propaganda campaigns in the mass media. Its activities are not regulated by laws, and are so covert that the ordinary citizen is rendered helpless.

By engaging in political persecution, the organs of interrogation and justice violate the rights of defendants guaranteed by Article 14 of the first agreement as well as by Czechoslovak law. Prisoners are treated in ways that demean their human dignity and are hurt both physically and morally.

Point 2 of Article 12 of the first pact, which guarantees the right to freely travel abroad is generally violated, the pretext being to "protect national security." Foreigners are often denied entry visas because they have been in contact with persons who have been discriminated against in our country.

Some citizens have privately and publicly drawn attention to these systematic violations of human rights and freedoms, and they have demanded redress in specific cases. However, either their voices have not been echoed or they themselves have been silenced by government investigations.

The responsibility for preserving civil rights naturally rests not only with the government but with each and every individual. Our belief in the sharing of responsibility, in the value of civic involvement, and in the need to find new and more effective forms of expression has prompted us to create Charter '77.

Charter '77 is a free, informal, and open community in which various convictions, religions, and professions co-exist. Its members are linked by the desire to work individually and collectively for human and civil rights in Czechoslovakia and the world. These rights are guaranteed by the final agreements of the 1975 Helsinki Conference and other international treaties against war, violence, and repression. Thus Charter '77 is based on the solidarity and friendship of all people who share a concern for certain ideals.

Yet Charter '77 is not an organization. It has no statutes, permanent organs, or registered membership. Everyone who agrees with its ideas and works to realize them belongs to it.

Charter '77 does not constitute an organized political opposition. It only supports the common good, as do many similar organizations that promote civic initiative in both the East and West. It has no intention of outlining specific and radical programs for political and social reform but tries instead to initiate a constructive dialogue with political and state authorities, particularly by drawing attention to specific violations of civil and human rights—by documenting them, suggesting solutions, submitting general proposals to ensure that these rights are respected in the future, and acting as a mediator in disputes between citizens and the state.

As signatories of this declaration, we entrust Dr. Jan Patočka, Dr. Václav Havel, and Professor Jiří Hájek to act as spokesmen for Charter '77. They are authorized to represent it before the state and other organizations, as well as before the public at home and abroad. Their signatures guarantee the authenticity of all Charter '77 documents.

We hope that Charter '77 will help to insure that all citizens of Czechoslovakia will someday live and work as a free people.

Prague,
January 1, 1977

2

Letters to Gustáv Husák,
Président and Secretary
General of the Central
Committee of the
Communist Party of
Czechoslovakia

The letters and appeals to Husák are not really meant to start a dialogue with him, for, since he was elected First Secretary of the Central Committee in April 1969, Husák has not answered a single letter that dared to criticize his regime. Still, every author here considers him politically responsible for the Soviet military occupation of August 21, 1968.

These letters can be divided into three categories. The most important ones are political statements. Some repeatedly remind the party leadership that current prominent officials actively participated in the reforms of 1968. A fact that is cited often is that Gustáv Husák himself was a victim of the show trials of the fifties. Milan Hübl speaks from his own experiences. He played a leading role in the fight to rehabilitate the victims of the show trials and was also a personal friend of Husák.

The authors, former functionaries who were expelled from the party, consider themselves spokesmen for a "socialist opposition" and insist that they represent political alternatives and are willing to make concrete proposals.

While the events of 1968 provide most of these letters with a point of departure, the playwright Václav Havel, one of the three spokesmen of Charter '77, has written a document that champions universal humanism, which is deeply rooted in Czechoslovak and European history. In reading his letter, one should keep in mind that Havel was never a socialist, although in 1968 he actively supported the reformers. The concerns that are expressed in his letter to Husák are also found in his plays.

In both he offers an analysis of the "language of puppets" in totalitarian regimes.

The second category of letters to Husák and the Party leadership is typified by Milan Hübl's. As a historian, he belongs to a profession that has been badly hurt by post-1968 repressive policies. These letters often refer to the personal experiences of their authors and were sent to Husák by the hundreds and thousands. Needless to say, they were not answered and did not improve the lot of their authors. The Party reacted to them with greater repression.

The third category is represented by appeals from relatives of political prisoners and are all addressed to Gustáv Husák himself. The right to petition is guaranteed by Czechoslovakia's Constitution. Article 29 says: "The citizen has the right to address propositions, proposals, and complaints to representative organs of the government and must be given a timely response."

All these letters and appeals were written at great personal risk to their authors; for those who criticize the Party and the government are inevitably declared criminals. These documents, only a few of which have appeared in the West, are proof of gross violations of human and civil rights in Czechoslovakia and testify to the awesome courage of the Czechoslovak people.

HANS-PETER RIESE

Milan Hübl to Gustáv Husák

Dear Comrade,

Despite the fact that my previous letter of February 12 has not been answered, I am writing to you again. I feel it important to communicate to you new facts, so that you will not be able to say one day that you were not informed in time.

Since July 1, 1970, the day I was suspended from the Party University, I have been unemployed. Since that day I have received no salary. I am not entitled to unemployment benefits and the stipend from the literary fund, for which I applied and to which I am entitled, has not been granted. I simply do not have any income.

For ten months I have been looking for work, but to no avail. I could not get a job in my profession as a historian nor any other work in Prague or Bratislava. Nobody is willing to hire me because I am on the "blacklist." The heads of various institutions are afraid to risk their own jobs by employing me. They know that the director of one institution who hired the former Prague secretary of the CPC has been dismissed.

I have worked in the Party apparatus since 1947, with the exception of the period of July 1964 to March 1968. If a private business were to treat an employee with twenty years seniority as I am treated, it would rightly be denounced as corrupt. If a Communist were unable to find work in France, no doubt the Communist Party would protest against political discrimination. So why is my fate regarded as normal, correct, and natural in a country that purports to be socialist?

You will, of course, refer to various statements made by other representatives of the present regime claiming that people who were punished by the Party still have the right to be employed according to their skills. I know of hundreds who were punished but not of a single person who is employed in compliance with official propaganda, unless, of course, you think that a doctor of science who was employed in research for twenty years and who now attends a water pump is properly placed, or that a professor of cybernetics or economics employed as an unskilled laborer is working at his profession. You are either misinformed about the present situation or you are lying to the public at home and abroad.

On October 1 my wife, Eliška Skřenková, lost her job as an assistant to the chairman of the Russian Studies department at the University. The head of the University had tried forcing her to resign by threatening to fire her because he had lost confidence in her. Since my wife was the only member of the family who was then employed, she refused to buckle under the threat, but Dean Otokar Taufer immediately fired her in the most ruthless way, citing the trumped-up charge. At the same time she was also expelled from the Party, the reason being that she "insisted that in 1968 we could have solved our problems by ourselves." This dismissal has made it impossible for her to find any kind of work.

My own chances of finding employment in these times of recession and discrimination against those who are not Party members are slim. To us the future holds out only one thing: denial of all means of subsistence. By the way, we are the parents of two children whom we must feed and educate.

A feeling of hopelessness has set in, and many have been driven to despair. In this situation, one understands why a poet lost his will to live when the Party betrayed the ideals for which he had joined it.

The lives of many people are being ruined. And yet, in violation of the Constitution you condone infringements upon the right to work and to defend one's honor. We are pariahs of society and any action against us is permitted. I do not exaggerate. All I have stated is true.

Not long ago a Soviet pamphlet entitled *Attention, Zionists* was published in a Slovak translation. Jevgenij Jevsejev wrote the afterword of the Czech edition. It has been widely distributed and is being used in Party lectures to educate the people about the fate of Zionism in 1968. The pamphlet was published by the Party's publishing house, and the afterword by *Východoslovenské noviny (East Slovakian News)*.

This tract accuses me of being one of the leaders of the "Zionist" movement in Czechoslovakia. When in the spring the *Trenčianské noviny (The Trencin News)* accused me of being one of the leaders of an international Zionist gang that gave lectures in Trencin—my lecture there was about the necessity for a new social order and the return of Husák to political life —I thought it was a joke. But now the "joke" is over. This country has already had its Dreyfus Affair in the "Hilsner story." Another far more bloody variant was the Slansky trial. Do you really want a third?

The aforementioned Jevsejev speaks of acts of espionage and sabotage worthy of the followers of Berija. He places me among members of a Zionist club, allegedly organized by an Israeli diplomat named Zucker. It would seem unnecessary to have to defend myself, since in a country without diplomatic relations with Israel, an Israeli diplomat could hardly function, much less organize anything. It would be pointless to prove that never in my life have I met or seen this Mr. Zucker. Or should I perhaps deny being a Zionist by proving that I am of Aryan origin? For Zionist experts of Jevsejev's ilk, it is enough to label one a Zionist if one's name has an umlauted vowel or if one has condemned the anti-Semitic trials of the fifties. Such people abide by the principle formulated by the old anti-Semite Lueger: "It is I who will decide who is a Jew." How humiliating that this goes on in a movement founded by Marx, Liebknecht, Luxemburg, and Lenin.

I ask whether the Party's statement of 1963 (that the trials of the fifties were contrived and that all who were indicted were innocent) still holds—considering how the government's weekly *Národní výbory (National Committees)* has reviewed this Soviet publication about Zionism seven times in succession, and the reviewer, Jaroslav Lang, has repeated the claim that a so-called anti-state conspiracy of Zionists was discovered and rightly punished. Moreover, the pamphlet itself has appeared in serial form in issues Nos. 34–50 of the same weekly. You look on as the Party and government press prepares a new round of political trials without showing the least concern. As early as September 25, 1969, I tried to let you know that a dangerous mechanism was being put into motion.

Are you unaware that the trial against the so-called Zionists is of a piece with the trial against the so-called Slovak nationalists? Everybody who knows how such trials are conducted can easily imagine how, in the first phase, for instance, I will be interrogated about my contacts with Zucker in the Kriegel Club, regardless of the fact that such a club does not exist and that I do not know Zucker. In the next phase, I may be forced to admit that I met with the Slovak conspirators in a club frequented by Husák. Investigators will no doubt have discovered that I often traveled to Bratislava and regularly visited "Obrancov mieru" and later Ostravska 4, the address of Husák's apartment. I may even have to speak of our joint appearances on TV and before the Kolodeje Commission.*

I do not mean to joke but only to stress that if you don't stop this campaign, it will overrun all of you in the end.

Let me conclude by reminding you that not too long ago we both fully agreed with Marx that "the revolution, which, like Saturn, devours its own children, has gone astray."

MILAN HÜBL
April 1972

*This Commission was instrumental in carrying out the rehabilitation of the victims of the show trials, one of whom was Gustáv Husák.

Václav Havel to Gustáv Husák

Dear Dr. Husák,

In our factories and offices, people work with determination. Their labor has resulted in the slow rise of our standard of living: People are building houses, buying cars, having children, and enjoying themselves. None of this reflects either the success or failure of your policy. After any period of unrest, people usually return to business as usual.

People are not restricting themselves to working, buying, and living according to their own fashion. They make special commitments to work, fulfill all expectations and even surpass them; they participate fully in elections and unanimously elect proposed candidates; they are active in different organizations and participate in meetings and demonstrations; they express their support for everything they are supposed to; nowhere may one find a single sign of disagreement with the government.

We cannot overlook these facts. We are forced to ask very earnestly if they are not proof that you have succeeded in realizing the program that you formulated—that is, to win the support of the people and to consolidate the country. The answer depends, of course, on how we understand the concept of consolidation.

If we allow that consolidation is reflected by statistics or official reports on the political activity of citizens, then nobody can question your success. But what if the concept means something more—say, the real inner state of a society? What if we begin to ask about other, more subtle, not easily quantifiable but nevertheless important things, which are confirmed by personal experience but are obscured by statistics and reports? What will we find when we direct our attention from mere external phenomena to their inner causes and effects? If we examine these deeper levels of reality, can we still regard our society as consolidated?

I assert beforehand that we cannot, that despite all the seemingly positive signs, our society is as divided as ever and is slipping into a crisis that in many respects is deeper than any other we have faced in recent history.

Let me try to prove my point. The fundamental question is why people behave the way they do. Why do they act in a way that creates the impression of a completely united society that fully supports its government? I think the answer is clear to any objective observer: fear is the reason. The teacher teaches what he does not believe because he fears losing his job, and fear for his future forces the pupil to learn; fear of being unable to continue their studies drives young people to join the Youth Association; fear that his son or daughter will not get enough points to be admitted to further studies compels the father to attend as many official functions as possible and "voluntarily" do everything that he is asked to do; fear of possible reprisals forces people to participate in elections, elect hand-picked candidates and act as if they really believe these rituals are real elections; fear for their life, position, or career compels them to vote for everything they are supposed to vote for, or at least to remain silent; fear weakens them into making humiliating self-criticisms and apologies and answer untruthfully demeaning questionnaires; fear that somebody may report them prevents them from expressing publicly or even privately their true views; fear that their lives will be made difficult drives workers to accept demeaning work and to form socialist workers' brigades, knowing beforehand that their praiseworthy activities will be reported to higher authorities; fear makes people attend official celebrations, demonstrations, and processions; fear that further work will become impossible forces many scientists and artists to accept ideas they don't believe in, write things against their wills or which they know to be untrue, join official organizations, take part in activities they despise, and destroy or deform their own creations. And in an attempt to save themselves, many denounce others for past activities, even when they themselves were accomplices.

The fear I am speaking about is not fear in the physiological sense, *i.e.*, a concrete emotion. The people we see around us are not trembling like aspen leaves but, rather, are quite satisfied and self-confident citizens. I am speaking of fear in a deeper sense: a more or less conscious collective awareness of a permanent and omnipresent threat. Everyone is worried about what is or could become a threat. Everyone slowly accepts feeling threatened as a norm and adapts to the situation in increasingly more natural and clever ways; for adaptation is the only way to survive. But fear, of course, is not the only thing our present social structure is founded upon. Nevertheless, it is and remains the most important element, without which it would have been impossible for Czechoslovaks to achieve the outward unity and discipline to which official documents refer and on which the government bases its claims of the consolidation of our society.

But what are the people afraid of? Of trials, torture, expropriation, deportation? No, none of these brutal forms of oppression survives in our society today. Repression nowadays is more subtle and selective; although there are still political trials, they represent only the most extreme danger. Now the main emphasis is on pressuring the individual's daily existence. This changes the rules of the game. It is known that the absolute value of a threat is not so important as its relative value. Now the issue is not what people can lose objectively but rather subjectively. This means that if somebody today is afraid that he may be unable to find work, his fear may be as strong and may lead him to the same actions that fear of property confiscation would have driven him to. The pressures on one's existence have in a certain sense become more universal: Everybody has something to lose and, therefore, reason to be afraid. The privileges of and possibilities open to the ruling elite, and the advantages that power affords, the opportunity to work or to pursue a career and the chance to make money, the opportunity to work at one's profession and to study, the prospect of living a secure existence and not falling among the victims of Czechoslovakia's apartheid—can all be lost. Yes, everybody has something to lose; even the unskilled worker can be forced to accept a lower-paying job in worse working conditions, and may have to pay a high price if he speaks out at a meeting or in a pub.

This system of intimidation could not function without the ever-present and omnipotent security police. Its network is a ghostly spider web covering the whole society, a web in which all lines of fear intersect. Although nobody can see or touch this invisible spider web, even the most simple-minded person is aware of its silent presence at all times and in all places, and behaves accordingly to avoid being interrogated, indicted, tried, and punished.

All decisions about one's fate are related in one form or other to the security police. Thus, the mere fact that the security police may at any time enter the life of a citizen—and there is no way to avoid this or to defend oneself against it—robs one of authenticity and forces one to play a perpetual charade.

Just as fear motivates attempts at self-preservation, so egotism and careerism account for aggressiveness in our society. It seems to me that seldom has a social system offered so blatantly the opportunity for everybody to confess whenever and to whatever he chooses, in order to gain personal privileges. The system offers advantages to people who lack principles and backbone, and who are willing to do anything for power and self-aggrandizement. These flunkies, for whom no self-humiliation is deep enough, always sacrifice honesty to please those in power. Thus it is no accident that so many high positions are occupied by well-known careerists, opportunists, swindlers, people of questionable past, and collaborators.

It is also no accident that corruption has reached its highest level in decades. Some officials are so corrupt that they are willing to accept bribes openly and for everything, and to be swayed by shameless and selfish motives. Fewer people than ever now believe official propaganda and support the government. Yet there are more and more hypocrites—every citizen, in a sense, is pressured to become a hypocrite.

This appalling situation has various causes. In the past the regime has seldom been interested in the real views and honesty of the outwardly loyal citizen. One has only to observe how nobody is interested in whether self-criticism or repentance is genuine or staged to gain some advantage. People are increasingly doing the latter without seeing anything immoral in it. Those who are forced or persuaded to make false statements are usually convinced that they have acted to save themselves. The beneficial results of such behavior are colorfully overstated and the bitter aftertaste that remains is trivialized.

One could say that in a certain way we are all bribed. If you perform certain functions at work that will benefit management, you will receive certain advantages. If you become a member of the Youth Association, you will receive the right and means to leisure time. If as an artist or writer you take part in official enterprises, you will be rewarded with certain creative opportunities. When you repress your desire for truth and your conscience, all doors will be opened wide for you.

Once the *principle of formal consent* has been accepted, which characteristics are encouraged in the individual and which are downplayed? Somewhere between a world dominated by fear and one ruled by selfishness exists a sphere we should never overlook because it helps to create the illusion of an "undivided society." This sphere is indifference and all its implications.

After the recent crises and stabilization of the country, our people seem to have lost their faith in the future—their faith that there is a possibility of bettering social conditions—and their hope that truth and right will prevail. They have abandoned everything that lies outside of their everyday, material worries, and they are looking for different ways of isolating themselves from society. They have fallen into apathy and have lost interest in universal values; they have slumped into spiritual passivity and depression. And those who try to combat this lethargy or who refuse to live a life of pretense are regarded as eccentrics, fools, and Don Quixotes.

Paradoxically, public indifference plays a very active role in our society. Is it not actually the case that many go to the election booths, to meetings, and join official organizations more out of indifference than out of fear? Is the seemingly smooth functioning of the political system not a matter of routine and convenience? What sense is there in not participating in all those political rituals which have no meaning but still afford at least some tranquillity? Most people do not like living in permanent conflict with their government, because they know they will lose in the end. And so they do what is asked of them without giving it a second thought. Thus hopelessness has led to apathy, apathy to adaptation, adaptation to automatic behavior—which is then seen as proof of the political activity of the masses.

The deeper the resignation that is felt by the individual and the greater chance he has to improve his own condition and relinquish universal values, the more he will direct his energy in the direction in which he will find the least resistance, *i.e.*, "inward." Thus, people are thinking far more intensely about themselves, their home and families. It is in this private sphere that they find peace and forget the stupidities of the world. They are concerned with home furnishings, beautiful things that will increase their standard of living and make life more pleasant. They build weekend houses and are preoccupied with food and clothing; in other words, they are concentrating primarily on the material things.

This orientation has had positive economic consequences. It accounts for the fact that the production of consumer goods and services is being speeded up; thus the standard of living is being raised. We possess a remarkable source of dynamic energy that partially meets the requirements for the creation of an affluent society—something the cumbersome and inefficient economy cannot ensure. For this reason the regime welcomes and supports this shift of energy from the public to the "private" sphere.

But why? Because it promotes economic development? No doubt this is part of the reason. The present propaganda machine supports this inconspicuous yet systematic "inward" turn because this psychological phenomenon represents an escape from social reality. The energy invested in satisfying private needs would otherwise be directed against the regime. Thus attention is purposefully being shifted from social concerns. The regime focuses the people's attention on pure consumer interests in order to prevent them from knowing to what degree they are spiritually, politically, and morally terrorized. The diminishment of a people into one-dimensional men who uphold the ideals of consumer society makes them pawns for so many manipulations. They are prisoners of narrowed horizons, the limited conditions of a centrally directed market.

All this proves that the regime behaves like an animal whose only goal is self-preservation. It tries to save itself from even the slightest resistance without regard to cost—a massive attack on human integrity and the brutal constriction of human beings.

The regime tries desperately to legitimize itself through its revolutionary ideology, which is founded on the notion of the free individual. But where is the Czechoslovak who develops his personality in a complex and authentic fashion, and is liberated from alienated social mechanisms, corrupt values, formal freedom, the dictatorship of the wealth, and the fetishistic power of money? Where is the Czechoslovak who experiences social and legal justice and participates willfully in the political process? Instead of participating in economic planning and in political life, and instead of freely developing their spirit, Czechoslovaks can only decide which refrigerator or washing machine to buy.

Thus the ideology of the Party apparently supports great humanistic ideals but in reality encourages the modest family life of the petty bourgeoisie! On the one hand we get bombastic slogans about the development of all kinds of freedoms, yet on the other all we have is a monstrous monotony and emptiness, a life reduced to the procurement of material things.

A secret and omnipotent power lurks behind the transformation of Czechoslovaks into an obedient herd of consumers: the state police. Everybody who has had the sad opportunity to find on himself its "handwriting" knows that the official explanation of its meaning is ridiculous. Or does anybody believe that the shady dealings of thousands of informers, professional undercover agents, and cunning petty bourgeois bureaucrats protect the nation and its achievements?

I believe that the only way to explain the grotesque contradiction between theory and practice is to see it as a natural consequence of the activities of our secret police, who frantically conduct a reign of terror and intimidation for the benefit of those who are threatened by the idea of the spiritual development of the individual.

The contradiction between revolutionary teachings about the new man and the new morality and the miserable conception of life as consumer happiness raises this question: Why does the regime stick so desperately to its ideology? Obviously, because the ideology—a system of rituals—gives legitimacy, continuity, and consistency to Party politics. The regime tries continually to manipulate the people with florid ideological phrases, which are hardly noticed because they have no instructive value. It issues pragmatic advice: "Don't concern yourself with politics; it is our cup of tea. Do only what we tell you to do, don't philosophize and interfere in business that does not concern you. Hold your tongue, do your work, and take care of yourself—and you will be happy."

And this advice is followed. The need to take care only of himself is the only point of agreement between the individual and the government. We are witnessing a gradual erosion of all moral norms, the devaluing of honesty, truth, steadfastness, unselfishness, dignity, and honor, which cannot lead to anything but life as vegetation, to that "depth of demoralization" that comes from the loss of hope and the feeling that life has no meaning. This collapse of moral values make us aware of the tragedy of man's condition in modern civilization—which derives ultimately from the disappearance of a concept of the Absolute. Yes, the government has created order, but by killing the spirit and deadening the heart of the Czechoslovak. An outward unification has taken place, but it has thrown our society into a *spiritual and moral crisis.*

The worst part is that this crisis is becoming more and more severe. One only has to look behind the trappings of daily life to see how fast we have embraced positions that even yesterday we condemned. What seemed dishonest is today excused; tomorrow it will be accepted as normal, and the following day, as an example of honesty. What we claimed we would never get accustomed to or what we simply thought to be impossible, we accept today without astonishment. And what was still natural a short time ago we regard today as an exception and—who knows—maybe in the near future as an unattainable ideal.

The change in the conception of what is "natural" and "normal" and the shift of moral norms that has taken place are greater than one would have thought. It is as if a disease had spread from the leaves and fruits of a tree to its trunk and roots.

A society develops, enriches, and cultivates itself by becoming more conscious of its successes and failures. And it is absolutely inevitable that when the development of the society is stunted by oppression, its culture will suffer. Cultural repression is not an automatic consequence of the social manipulation of spirit but is something programed that results from the justified fear that through culture a society becomes aware of its failures.

Through culture, society extends its freedom and discovers truth. Thus what interest in culture can a society have that is based on the suppression of truth? Such a society recognizes only one "truth," the one that suits it. And only one "freedom" is recognized, the freedom to express this "truth."

A world which springs not from dialectical interactions but from the brutal exercise of power by a few, harbors sterility of thought and stubborn dogmatism. It is a world of prohibitions, limitations, and orders. A world in which culture is determined by the police.

Much has already been said and written about the remarkable degree to which our present culture has been devastated: Hundreds of writers, books, and dozens of magazines and newspapers have been banned. The publishing industry and the theater have been crippled, galleries have been pillaged, and organizations of artists and scientific institutions are run by aggressive partisans, infamous careerists, and ambitious cowards. I do not intend to belabor this point. I will simply reflect on some aspects of this situation which are connected with the theme of my letter.

First, however bad the situation is, it does not mean that culture does not exist. The theaters are open, television programs are on the air every day, and books are being published. These official, legal, and cultural activities have one thing in common: shallowness. This shallowness originates in the alienation of culture from its essential task, which is to increase human and social self-awareness. Nowadays when something undoubtedly valuable appears on the cultural scene—for instance, an outstanding performance by an actor—it is tolerated only if it is subtle. But as soon as it tries overtly to raise the people's consciousness, the regime begins instinctively to defend itself. There are known cases where a good actor has been banned because he was too good.

I am interested in how this cultural alienation manifests itself in those areas where human experience is depicted most clearly. Let us suppose that a literary work is published or a play that seems rich in ideas and meaning is performed skillfully. This sometimes happens. Yet, however different such works may be, they have one thing in common: they never transcend the conventional or the banal. Thus they reflect false social consciousness. It does not matter whether they do so because of censorship, self-deception, or resignation. They replace authentic world experience with a superficial and harmless semblance, a dead shadow of experience, which the social consciousness has for a long time accepted as the real thing.

Despite this—or to be more precise, because of this—such art may be amusing, moving, interesting, and exciting to many, but it does not shed light on the unknown, does not declare what was previously left unsaid, and does not reveal—in new, distinctive, and effective ways—the subconscious. Such art falsifies the real world because it imitates the real world.

This esthetic of the banal relies on petty bourgeois morality, the sentimentality of the housemaid, and the vulgarity of simple, happy endings. Its backbone is benign mediocrity and moldy complacency. Ultimately, it encourages false optimism and lamely insists that "truth will prevail."

There are very few artistic works that openly support the ideology of the government, and these are technically very poor. Still, sometimes they open old wounds and provoke general reactions by their radical political character. What I call the esthetics of banality serves the interests of the present leadership far better. It skirts the truth more neatly, pleasantly, and inconspicuously, and is accepted by the social consciousness far more readily. Naturally, works of this kind were always in the majority, but some, which in one way or other communicated the possibility of authentic human self-realization, always penetrated into the public domain. These succeeded, though seldom immediately, in increasing social awareness.

This seems to me to be the most important thing: For the first time since our national renaissance in the eighteenth century, the government has succeeded in surpressing serious artistic works. The censorship of culture is so effective that not even the tiniest gaps through which an important word could slip out exist. A small group has the keys to culture in their pockets. Not only is there a voluminous index of totally or partially banned authors and artists but something far worse: the a priori banning of any original idea and suggestive art form. A warrant has been issued in advance against anything with a critical edge.

Where does all this lead? What will become of our society?

The majority of cultural journals that once appeared are no longer published. The few that still exist are so conformist that they are not worth reading. What is the consequence? At first glance, nothing. Our society keeps functioning without these journals devoted to literature, the arts, theater, philosophy, history, and other realms of culture. Even when they existed, they did not meet the latent needs of Czechoslovaks. But they played a role in our lives. How many citizens miss these publications today? Only about ten thousand subscribers, a very small part of the population.

Nevertheless, the loss is far greater than these figures reveal. The real importance of this loss is hidden and cannot be qualified. The banning of a magazine—say, of a theater revue —is not only of concrete disadvantage to readers, and a severe blow to the theater, but is the elimination of an organ that keeps the multifaceted organism that is Czechoslovakia alive. It is harmful to the natural, dynamic processes of the social organism and disrupts its equilibrium. How great will the damage be if not just one but all magazines are banned?

The free space of spiritual self-realization is indivisible. Once a thread is cut, the net is ruined. There is an interconnectedness of all the subtle processes of the social organism. The fact that in the past few years not a single novel has appeared in the bookstores that could have widened the horizons of our people will have sad consequences. Who knows how this void will affect the spiritual and moral climate of Czechoslovakia in the next few years? To what extent will our abilities "to know something about ourselves" diminish? How will such a lack of cultural references affect those who are just beginning to see themselves for what they really are? How many mystifications will have to be cleared up? Who knows when and where someone will find the strength to light a new flame, once not only the opportunity but the feeling that it is possible are lost?

A few books missing from the bookstores do exist and are distributed in manuscript form. The situation, therefore, is not entirely hopeless. Even if only twenty people read them, they are still important for all the reasons I have given.

Still, I am afraid that present political interests will stifle culture for many years to come. And those who have sacrificed the future of their nation for power must bear the historical responsibility.

A basic law of the universe is the entropy of all things; but life is always striving toward more complex structures and therefore fights entropy. Life defends itself against uniformity. It is governed by the principle of differentiation. Life is the rebellion against the status quo.

In contrast to the flux of life, political power wants to remain unchanged. Such power has a deep-rooted suspicion of diversity, individuality, and transcendence; an aversion to everything that is unknown, intangible, and mysterious, and a desire for uniformity and immutability. It substitutes the inert for the living and is not at all concerned with higher forms of social organization.

In human life there is a moment when the body begins to fail and entropy takes over, and a moment when man finally succumbs to this universal law, and dies. Similarly, power follows the course of entropy by turning human beings into automatons and brings about its own destruction. The "order" that power tries to realize reeks of death. For from its point of view, every individual act, personal expression, unique thought, unpredictable desire or idea inevitably signals "confusion," "chaos," "anarchy." This all applies to the present regime and its policies, the chief features of which I have tried to describe. The ideas of "silence," "order," "consolidation," "overcoming the crisis," "arresting the decomposition," "soothing the passions" were from the very start the basis of the regime's political program and are, in the final analysis, deadly. In our country there is order and silence, but the order and silence of a mortuary or grave.

In a society that is really alive, something is always happening. Open and hidden motions create new and unique situations which in turn create others. There, the dialectic of the constant and the changing, lawfulness and anarchy, and the predictable and the unexpected, unfolds in daily events. And a society that is alive has a history. But because in history, continuity and causality are closely connected with uniqueness and unpredictability, a new question arises: How is real history—this permanent "chaos," this rage against order—to be understood in a world ruled by "timeless" regimes?

The answer is clear. History bogs down in such a world. So it is that in Czechoslovakia, history seems to have come to a standstill. Slowly our sense of the past is diminishing. Everything is getting blurred and is turning into a picture of sameness. Thus we say "nothing has happened."

The confusion of history's chronological order leads inevitably to the confusion of private life. As the background of society and of the individual is lost, private life is absorbed by the timeless rhythms of birth, marriage, and death. Moreover the disorder of real history is replaced by the order of a pseudo-history. Instead of real events, pseudo-events are staged: We live from anniversary to anniversary, from celebration to celebration, from parade to parade, from one unanimous Party conference to a unanimous election, from the "day of the press" to "the day of the military." And while these rituals had a deep existential meaning for our ancestors, for us they are only a routine, an end in themselves. Thus society is put in a strait jacket and becomes one dimensional.

Now, in its attempt to create a timeless world, the regime itself stagnates, and its ability to confront new facts and resist progress diminishes. Thus it is forced by its own essence to become a victim of entropy, the deadly principle. And it is vulnerable because its own nature deprives it of the motivation to defend itself against itself.

Tyranny can suppress life only so long as some life exists. Power is existentially dependent on life, though life not on power. The only force that could destroy life on our planet is a power that brooks no compromise. And as long as life cannot be definitively destroyed, it is impossible to bring history to a complete standstill. Sooner or later a small, secret, mysterious stream of life, which flows slowly and inconspicuously, will break through the heavy cover of rigidity and pseudo-progress.

Then, something will begin to happen, something new and unique that was never officially planned, but which will rescue us from indifference, something in which we will hear the voice of history. And what will its message be?

I am neither a historian nor a prophet. Still, there are some things that cannot be overlooked.

When the struggle for power takes place in the open and freedom of speech exists, the public can check the advances of the power-hungry. Whether the powerful want to or not, they have to participate in a permanent and open dialogue with the people, and have to deal constantly with social problems. When the struggle for power is covert, the powerful do not try to adapt themselves to life but try to adapt life to themselves. This means that instead of solving real problems and contradictions, they simply conceal them. Nevertheless, the contradictions and problems exist; they accumulate and grow and soon explode.

The regime may still have enough strength to resist some pressures arising from the contradictions of life, but it does not have enough power to resist all.

Thus life fights power. It forces power to start secret discussions and to struggle for its existence. Power starts to panic. Life causes confusion among the leaders in the form of personal conflicts and intrigues. And then the death masks suddenly disappear and real people who fight against each other for power appear on the scene.

This is the moment when revolutions occur, and sudden changes in personal and political positions take place. This is the moment when real and alleged conspiracies are discovered, real or invented crimes are publicized, old sins are excavated, cliques are formed, and politicians smear and imprison each other. Until this moment, all representatives of power will have spoken the same language, used the same phrases, and recited the same goals. Now suddenly the monolithic power block will disintegrate into lone individuals. We will be able to differentiate between them. We will be surprised to hear that those who have fallen were never concerned with the proper goals, only those who have triumphed were.

For years the regime has down-played the unique and unpredictable, but in one single moment, a secret, hidden for years, will break through. All of us will experience a big surprise. The whole "disorder" of history, suppressed by an artificial order, will resume. A mechanism that will have worked apparently smoothly for so many years, without variations and complications, will go to pieces in a single night. A group that created the impression that it would remain in power until the end of the world, because no force could challenge it in this world of unanimous elections, will suddenly be disbanded. And we will be surprised to find that everything is different from what we thought.

This upheaval will by no means be amusing to those of us outside the power structure. It will affect us, though indirectly; it will revive us. We should not be surprised if our society wakes up again. Such an upheaval nearly always creates new hopes and worries, and different social problems. Risks are involved.

When the volcano of life erupts and rational efforts to undo injustice and realize truth are made, we will also see outbreaks of hatred, malice, and vengeance. It is no wonder that the regime, accustomed for years to unconditional support of the people, will panic. They will feel threatened and menaced, and will protest that only they can guarantee the continued existence of the world. They will not hesitate to ask for the help of foreign armies for their own safety and that of the world.

Recently we experienced such an upheaval. The very same leaders, who humiliated and offended the people for years, were shocked when the people wanted to speak out; they called it "an explosion of passions." But which passions actually did explode? Those who know the many humiliations suffered by the people must be surprised at how relatively quiet, objective, and even loyal this "explosion" was.

We will have to pay a high price for the next "hour of

truth." The present regime is fundamentally different from the one that preceded it. The former leadership could rely on the faithful support of the people and on their acceptance of its policies. The present regime cannot. As a ruling minority it is motivated entirely by its instinct for self-preservation and by its fear of the majority.

At the moment it is difficult to imagine all the possible alternatives that will open up during the "hour of truth." One can hardly imagine what reparations will be demanded for past humiliations suffered by the people. And one cannot at all imagine how tragic this hour will be.

This letter, therefore, reveals what I am afraid of: the senseless and long-lasting consequences of the oppression of Czechoslovaks. I am afraid of the price we will have to pay in casting it off.

I hope it is clear that I am not so worried about the bitterness the people feel regarding their rape and humiliation, nor about the high toll we are paying in the form of spiritual and moral decline: I am worried about the price we as a people will have to pay once we come into our own.

The responsibility for the state of the nation may vary among leading politicians. Nobody rules by himself. Some of it must also be shared by those who influence the leaders. No country lives in a vacuum. Its policy is always influenced in one way or another by the policy of other countries. Many, therefore, share the blame, including all citizens. Each individual has contributed to the present situation by his daily actions and decisions.

Nonetheless, Dr. Husák, your responsibility for the state of affairs is very great. You had the decisive word in the creation of the climate in which we all live. We are able to develop our creativity, do unexpected spiritual and moral deeds, and also sacrifice ourselves for others and fight for our freedom, but we are also capable of total indifference and of not being interested in anything that is not material.

For the time being you have chosen to promote what is most convenient for you but most dangerous for the society: outward prosperity at the cost of inner decay, and your own power at the cost of our spiritual and moral decline.

But you have the ability to improve the situation if only in a limited way. As a citizen of this country, I am publicly calling on you and all the other leaders of the present regime to consider the issues I have brought to your attention and live up to your responsibility.

VÁCLAV HAVEL
April 8, 1975

An Appeal by Relatives of Political Prisoners

Mr. President,

We invoke the Czechoslovak Constitution and in its name request that you, in accordance with your responsibilities, set free our sons, husbands, and children, who are imprisoned because of their socialist convictions and activities. At the same time we demand that you heed our complaints against their living conditions, which violate the international treaty on human and political rights and also the laws concerning the execution of sentences. These conditions do physical damage and cause psychological breakdowns.

The accommodations: Although our relatives have received the lightest punishments, they are actually living in the worst conditions. Each has been forced to live in a small cell measuring roughly 2 yards by 4 with one other prisoner, who is usually apolitical. Living with another person twenty-four hours a day can become an unbearable burden. And conversations are taped by prison officials.

The sensory experience of our relatives is very limited; their world is stripped of natural colors, sounds, and other stimuli. This lack of stimulation and forced companionship can all but destroy a human being.

Work: Prisoners work in their cells. They sew buttons on garments, sort safety pins, hair pins, buttons, and glass pearls, make artificial flowers, make chairs, and perform other similar tasks. The common features of this type of work are monotony, a quick pace, and long hours (ten to twelve hours per day). If his work-quota is not met, the prisoner is punished—for instance, by taking away some of his meals. Circumstances beyond the prisoner's control are not taken into account.

The law requires that health and ability be taken into consideration when allocating work to prisoners, and that opportunities for self-improvement be provided. Czech political prisoners are mostly university graduates (in history, economics, psychology, sociology, design, medicine, etc.). Their skills can hardly be used in prisons.

The wages of political prisoners are not even one-half the wages of regular convicts, and amount to one-fifth of the average wage in Czechoslovakia. Nevertheless, the prison command deducts approximately 80 percent for maintenance. The prisoner receives between 20 and 40 kronen per month, which is the only money he has to supplement his meals. He is not permitted to receive money from his relatives. We see a complex form of exploitation involving the fixing of quotas and wage deductions. These working conditions resemble those of serfdom and are unconstitutional.

Health care: Those who leave prison come home in poor health and have to convalesce for some time. Their eyesight has suffered great damage. Some are very sick. The health of prisoners is ruined by the lack of fresh air, the restriction of exercise, poor hygenic facilities, and the lack of proteins, vitamins, and minerals in their diet. Prison food violates all rules of proper nutrition. Once every three months, prisoners can receive a care package of up to three kilograms, but this cannot replace what their diet lacks.

Only reluctantly do prison officials provide medical care, and the advice of physicians is disregarded in most cases. Medical treatment is of actual complaints and not preventive.

The situation of the prisoner and his family: Although the court sentences only the prisoner, his whole family is punished as well. His children may visit him for only four hours per year; in most cases, they are not even allowed to touch him. One prison visit lasting one hour is permitted quarterly, and only two visitors may attend. Prison officials generally arrange these visits in large halls.

Prison guards know that visits and correspondence help a prisoner maintain his integrity and are a source of strength. Since 1973 each prisoner is allowed to write only one letter per week. The letters are often returned to the prisoner for rewriting because a sentence was "objectionable," or the writing was "poor." The letters we relatives write are often confiscated and our imprisoned relatives have no chance to read them. Some letters are lost quite mysteriously. This censorship is humiliating and senseless. Letters are not supposed to mention books, movies, the work of the prisoner, or that of his free relatives. It is forbidden to write poems; no Czech authors may be mentioned. There is no appeal against this censorship.

The families of prisoners are economically deprived. In most cases the family loses its breadwinner, and his spouse, mother, and other close relatives are either fired or demoted. The children are not permitted to attend high schools or universities. Their basic needs are not met. This discrimination against children is prohibited by both the Czechoslovak Constitution and the international pact on civil and political rights.

The special status of political prisoners and the system of intimidation: In any other country, our imprisoned relatives would have the official status of "political prisoners" because they were tried for their political activities and defense of human rights.

In Czechoslovakia the status of "political prisoner" is not officially recognized. According to the law, political prisoners are simply "people taken into custody in compliance with Chapter I of the special provision of the penal code." Thus, our relatives do not enjoy the rights that are granted to political prisoners in other societies. Our relatives not only don't enjoy the privileges that are accorded to criminals but are treated in a worse manner.

The basic trend in the treatment of political prisoners since 1968 has been to make violence and torture less frequent. The penal system wanted to both keep its distance from Stalinism and exercise its ability to wear down the prisoner. Thus, in line with our "cultural tradition," bloodless methods were introduced (though they were not painless). More sophisticated methods were invented, like putting a healthy man in a mental institution and having drops of water fall regularly on the neck of a prisoner, causing him to go mad.

The imprisonment of Czech political prisoners has some special features. Lack of care is a less conspicuous but not less cruel form of punishment than direct physical assault. In this situation of helplessness and suffering, prisoners invest normal things with the importance of life or death. A dim bulb in a dark cell, a hard workbench, and ten to twelve hours of work a day for weeks, months, and years, become new instruments of torture. Torture is certainly being practiced when a sick prisoner with tumors and abscesses all over his body (for lack of vitamins) is given a wooden plank to sleep on.

Intellectual isolation is also a form of psychological torture. The rigorous limitations placed on sensual experience by the monotony of cell life make a human being feel very intensely the need for excitement, information, and pictures from the outside world. The spirit of our imprisoned relatives is intentionally being deadened. In some prisons, inmates may read per week only one newspaper and one book, which are selected by the prison guard. It often happens that the same book is assigned over and over to the same cell. (Most of the books are either by Stalinists or by Czech writers of the nineteenth and twentieth centuries.) Our relatives are forbidden to read any foreign or professional literature, or to consult foreign grammar books and dictionaries. Even Marxist literature is banned. It is prohibited to take notes or excerpts. All unauthorized reading matter is confiscated.

One part of "prison culture" is forced listening of prison broadcasts; every fortnight the prisoner is brought for two hours into a cell with one table, four chairs, and a TV set. The time allotted to him for viewing is strictly regulated; once it is over, the prisoner is returned to his cell. In many instances he sees only parts of different programs. Our relatives are also denied creative work. The "bugging" of their cells forces them to keep their thoughts to themselves for endless hours.

Jailers arbitrarily mistreat prisoners for even the most trifling "offenses." The whole system is designed to intimidate the prisoner and to make him believe that he has no rights and is subject to the whims of his jailer.

The recognition of the absurdity of his imprisonment stifles the spiritual development of the prisoner. Human beings need to feel that life has meaning, and this need prompted our relatives to make those decisions and to take those actions for which they were imprisoned. Now that their daily work lacks all meaning, they have become depressed.

Complaints, defense: We trust our fellow citizens and we believe that among the prison guards and personnel there are those whose objectivity prevails over unjust prejudices. We ask their help. The basic injustice remains that those who have been imprisoned are neither criminals nor terrorists. Honest and highly educated people have been jailed because they fought for their own civil rights and those of their fellow citizens, and did it by means that are in accord with the international agreements on human rights, which our government has promised to respect.

Although our relatives suffer injustices at the hands of jailers who do not compare with them either intellectually or morally, they have not been defeated: They have succeeded in maintaining calm, dignity, courage, and faith.

We are asking for their immediate release and invoke the Final Act of the Conference for Security and Cooperation that was signed by the Czechoslovak Socialist Republic in Helsinki.

> VILÉM MÜLLER, FRANTIŠKA MÜLLEROVÁ,
> MARIE RUSKOVÁ, IVAN RUSEK,
> TAT'ANA RUSKOVÁ, ANNA ŠABATOVÁ,
> JAN ŠABATA, ELIŠKA SKŘENKOVÁ (HÜBLOVÁ),
> VÁCLAV ŠABATA, JANA TESAŘOVÁ.
> Prague, Brno
> *March 1, 1976*

3

Letters and Appeals to Various Political Institutions and Leaders

These letters and appeals addressed to various Czechoslovak political institutions are the best proof we have of how the resistance movement maintains its legality. The list of addresses includes institutions like the Parliament, the Czech and Slovak National Council, the highest branches of the government, and the Supreme Court. This form of letter writing developed because people felt that conventional legal channels were blocked. For instance, the national press often publishes defamations of critics of the regime who, by law, have committed punishable offenses. Every one of the victims could present whole files of replies and self-justifications. Some have tried to go to court. Yet, in not a single case have legal procedures been brought against the press, though there is ample proof of the inaccuracy of the reports in the press. In other cases, legal action was delayed and sometimes permanently "delayed" in the lower courts.

Pavel Kohout is someone who has been denied due process in the courts, and he charges the regime with practicing "apartheid."

Former Party chief, Alexander Dubček, describes the intimidation and terrorization of citizens by the secret police in a moving letter addressed to the Parliament. As in all totalitarian countries, there is no appeal against the secret police. It is everywhere and acts when it feels the need. Dubček describes its omnipresence as a "spider web," covering the whole country, whose sole function is to secure the personal power of Party functionaries.

In nearly all these letters there are hints that not only the victims of "apartheid" are exposed to suffering but also their friends and relatives. This increase in repression aims at increasing the isolation of critics of the regime and leads to a prisonlike situation even for people who are free.

These letters have provoked reactions from the Party leaders that prove the cogency of their arguments. The letter from Dubček to Husák was particularly effective. Husák responded to it in a speech on April 6, 1975, that was published the next day in *Rudé právo*. First, Husák tried to defend his policy: "After April 19 we decided to solve problems not administratively but politically. I think that this decision was correct. We solved them in a humane way according to our world view." The extent to which this statement does not reflect the real facts is shown in Dubček's letter. Husák must have been alarmed by the fact that it was Dubček who broke the silence, and thus he gave the impression of wishing to avoid something.

He recommended emigration to his predecessor: "Dubček should pack his suitcases tomorrow and leave. . . . He has chosen the bourgeois way, the way of international reactionaries. Let him go." Though this letter had circulated among small groups, it awakened the curiosity of most people only after it was mentioned in Husák's speech.

In April 1975 house searches and imprisonments took place throughout the whole country, particularly in Prague. On this occasion a strange and tragic confiscation occurred. Thousands of pages of notes by the philosopher Karel Kosík were confiscated. This prompted him to write to Jean-Paul Sartre. Foreign magazines, like *Der Spiegel*, and books were taken from others. So was a copy of a 250-page analysis of the reform policy which was written by Zdeněk Mlynář and was supposed to have been sent to the Berlin summit. Then suddenly the confiscations stopped. Some of the material that was taken by force, including Mlynář's manuscript, was returned; no indictments were issued. It appears that the regime wanted to intimidate individuals rather than engage in general repression.

The year of the Conference on Security and Cooperation in Europe, 1975, saw increased activity among critics of the regime. The pile of letters and appeals addressed to the government grew. More and more reform Communists surfaced. Concrete proposals and suggestions were offered. The demand for fulfillment of the Helsinki principles intensified. The atomic scientist,

František Janouch, made proposals for liberalizing the penal code in Czechoslovakia, particularly the infamous paragraphs 98 and 100, the basis of nearly all political trials in Czechoslovakia. And since 1969 well-known functionaries like Zdeněk Mlynař, František Kriegel, and Jiří Hájek have been discussing reform Communism and have begun to hint at the emergence of Eurocommunism.

The police did not succeed in silencing any of these critics. The more repressive the government became, the more the solidarity of critics of the regime grew, resulting ultimately in Charter '77.

The final call to action came in August 1975 during the trial of Plastic People of the Universe and DG 307, two well-known rock bands in Prague. The police accused them of singing obscene lyrics, inciting youth to rebel against the socialist society, and—what is a peculiarity of the penal code in nearly all socialist states—of being hippies. The trial was such an obvious farce that many prominent writers and intellectuals defended the musicians and wrote an open letter to Heinrich Böll. One of the initiators of this letter was Jan Patočka, a professor of philosophy. Although he himself is not a supporter of pop music, Patočka went so far as to approach the general prosecutor.

The Charter is the culmination of the Czechoslovak protest movement; the reaction it elicited from the regime was never more severe. In its press campaign against the the signatories of the Charter, the regime even began to use language that is reminiscent of the fifties.

Signatories were threatened with reprisals. The secret police went to work: telephones were cut off, many signatories were fired from their jobs, apartments had to be vacated, and many were taken into custody. One spokesman and two signatories, the playwright Václav Havel, the journalist Jiří Lederer, and the director Fratišek Pavliček, were imprisoned.

Charter '77 demonstrates that when the opposition in Czechoslovakia uses the principle of legality—even going so far as to deny being an opposition at all—it is most effective.

Hans-Peter Riese

To the Czechoslovak Citizenry

We have been asked to participate in the November elections. The regime needs us to act as millions of puppets to achieve "consolidation."

The regime is not sure of how the youngest voters will behave at the polls and have doubts even about the rest of the population. Therefore they want to turn the elections into a farce in which all voters will be forced to vote for the hand-picked candidates, thereby sanctioning the occupation and the abolition of civil rights. Government officials will stigmatize as an enemy of socialism anyone who does not participate in the elections.

It is clear that these elections will be a fraud, for their outcome has already been determined. We are not allowed to choose our representatives in the Parliament, the county districts, and the local people's councils.

Nevertheless, whether we vote or cross out the names of candidates is important. The election committees must give a report of how many voters boycotted the elections and how many voted against official candidates. We must register our disapproval of present conditions in Czechoslovakia that result from the occupation by foreign troops. International affairs show that the Soviet Union respects only those who defend their own point of view, and we should bear in mind that the rest of the world will not forget us, as long as we continue to remind it of our fate. Others will not give up on us if we don't give up on ourselves!

1. Not to participate in the elections is the most open way to demonstrate disapproval of present policy. To take part in the election is not a duty but a right, and each citizen must decide for himself whether to exercise this right. He cannot be punished for not voting; the government can only note his action in his cadre files. The propagandists do not represent state organs; they have no right to force anybody to vote. Each citizen is free to decide whether he will allow them to enter his apartment or refuse them as unwanted guests.

2. The law states that all elections should be by secret ballot; so-called "demonstrative voting" is not part of the law. Paragraph 34 of the election law provides for election booths ("rooms in which to fill out ballots"). And because all elections are supposed to be by secret ballot, these booths must be designed so that the voters will have privacy. Please see to it that these conditions are observed, regardless of whether or not you want to cross out names; the issue is respect for the law.

3. To vote against a candidate requires that his whole name, first and last, be crossed out. According to rules which the election committees must respect, if his name is not completely crossed out, you have, in effect, voted for him. If you merely write on the ballot, the commission will still count it as a valid vote. In small communities it is permitted to vote for decent local candidates and cross out the names of candidates for higher offices. It is possible to put in the envelope, instead of the crossed-out ballot, one's own proposals, or write on the ballot the motto: "Prague Spring yes, occupation no!—the Socialist Movement of Czechoslovak Citizens."

Dr. František Janouch to the Chief Justice of the Supreme Court

Dear Sir:

It was with great uneasiness that I read fragmentary reports of the political trials that took place in the summer of this year.

I became convinced that Czechoslovak laws have been bent in these trials and that innocent people were sentenced. I refer particularly to the trial of Dr. Šabata, Dr. Hübl, Dr. Tesař, and Mr. Litera, and those who were tried with them.

Let me substantiate my position:

1. The trials took place behind closed doors. Not even a public announcement of the sentence was permitted. The incomplete reports in the mass media concealed more than they revealed of the defendants' "offense", views, defense, and attitudes. This contradicts one of the basic tenets of socialism: the free and open discussion of public issues.

Since all the defendants were Communists who were active in the 1968 reform movement, I wonder whether they were not tried for their activities during the Prague Spring. The policies of the Prague Spring are shared by many in the international Communist movement. A socialist court should not operate in a manner that arouses such suspicions as mine, especially since the ideals of the Prague Spring are shared by so many people throughout the world.

2. Paragraph 98 of the penal code requires that the court determine the criminal's motives as well as the evidence of a punishable act. I am convinced that in these trials, motive was not and could not have been proved. I happen to know that all the defendants are devout Communists and Marxists; they have proved their convictions over the years not only with words but also with deeds. To accuse them of being enemies of a socialist system is as absurd as similar accusations that were leveled in the fifties against R. Slánský, J. Frank, Dr. Husák, and L. Novomeský.

I suppose that in these trials *critical* attitudes toward some aspects of our system were identified with *hostility* to socialism in general.

I feel I should remind you that different paths to socialism are acknowledged by Marxist doctrine, a fact that was often emphasized by Lenin and, more recently, in 1969 in Moscow at the Conference of Communist and Workers Parties. Our legislators knew this when they drew up the penal code. Therefore, anyone who criticizes aspects of our socialist system, offers suggestions to improve and perfect it, and looks to new models, can under no circumstance be deemed "hostile" to the state. Real hostility must be proved in order to apply paragraph 98 of the penal code. Further, it is well known that according to Marxist dialectic philosophy, any development is to be seen as growing out of contradictions. If our courts now sentence Communists and Marxists because they have different views on some theoretical and practical issues concerning the development of socialism, then surely the dialectic has bogged down and progress is being impeded.

Therefore, Mr. Chief Justice, I propose that the Supreme Court repeal the sentences meted out at these trials, or allow the filing of appeals.

Sincerely,
DR. FRANTIŠEK JANOUCH CSC
Prague
August 20, 1972

Pavel Kohout to Milan Klusák, Minister of Culture of the Czech Socialist Republic

Dear Sir,

Leading European writers like Böll, and many Communist writers like Aragon, claim that artistic works are being destroyed in our country and that their creators are being persecuted. They are right. My colleague, the English writer James Aldridge, states the opposite. He is wrong.

The balance sheet of official Czech culture has no parallel. Poetry is reduced to two or three names. Not a single prose work of importance has been published. Not a single play has been produced that compares well with any of 1969. After the banning of outstanding performances of such plays as *Mother Courage* by Brecht and the closing of the *Theater Behind the Gate*, not a single play has contributed to the development of the theater. Even experienced film artists who represent Barandov, the film center in Prague, are unable to make movies dealing with the problems and conflicts of our times that are worthy of comparison with those of the late Jan Procházka. And after visiting the great exhibition in the Cavalry School of the Prague Castle, one laments the fact that outstanding pictures, graphics, and sculptures cannot be seen by everyone. Czech musical culture is represented in the world by a few soloists and orchestras with rigid repertoires and by pop singers who changed their protest songs of 1968 to conform to the new political situation.

There is no doubt that the cultural policy of your predecessor proved to be a complete failure. The tiny group of artists who defend themselves by claiming a lifelong inability to say "no" has been joined in latter years by small talents, people who were willing to give up their own views in order to survive or facilitate the upbringing of their children. Membership in the organizations of artists brings unbelievable material advantages but at the same time does great moral harm: The organizations are instruments of discrimination, and the majority are as far removed from art as from socialism.

After disbanding the old artists' organizations, whose representatives were elected by secret ballot, the new leadership declared that it would take Czech culture out of the hands of cliques and power groups. Yet the number of active artists in all creative fields has diminished. Certain members and functionaries have a virtual monopoly on artistic activity. They gloat over the fact that the majority of artists have been silenced, and they do everything in their power to prolong this silence.

Only in repressive times could theater reviews and the novel *Shadows of the Cathedral* be published by an uneducated dilettante, who is as ideologically suspect as his fantastic career from cleric to newly registered member of the Party and who has replaced expelled prewar Communists. Only now could a hack, whose works such as *Your Hour Won't Come* would never under normal circumstances have been performed by even a struggling young theater, become one of the most popular Czech playwrights. Only now is it possible for some parks in Prague to exhibit more and more sculptures that offend all artistic sensibilities.

If a director wants to employ a prominent and beloved actor, he must also employ some functionaries and activists of the Artists Union as well. The latter are very often of below-average talent but nevertheless find opportunities to perform in movies and on TV. Also, the top positions in publishing houses, theaters, orchestras, agencies, and other cultural institutions are for the most part given to Union members. These are mostly people who over the years have failed to achieve any artistic distinction, yet nevertheless have been entrusted with the education of young artists. Union prizes and other awards are exchanged among the leadership.

The general decline of artistic values reached its nadir with the TV series *The Rainbow,* which is notorious for its stupidity, verbosity, and tastelessness, and was hastened by the banning of hundreds of Czech authors. As a result, the future generation of Czech readers will get a completely distorted picture of our national literature. (I wrote in my last letter to your predecessor that I have a so-called "List of Trashy Literature No. 1" that was prepared by his Ministry for all state libraries in Czechoslovakia, and it includes 152 names of Czechoslovak writers, historians, economists, etc., whose entire works have been banned.)

This censorship has affected not only Czech but also Soviet art. Publishing houses, theaters, concert halls, and television have replaced seemingly "apolitical" art with politically committed art. But "apolitical" art is not as frivolous as it is made out to be but often deals critically with the problems of socialism. There are big sales of Soviet art at greatly reduced prices. There are weeks when the number of Soviet productions shown on television, in theaters, and at the movies, is far greater than our own. Aside from the fact that this leads to a politically intolerable disproportion, ours runs the risk of becoming a second- or third-rate culture.

In your first TV interview with the representatives of artists' associations, you hinted that you had consented to be interviewed in order to open them up to all serious artists. But you repeated the view of your predecessor in saying that you are unwilling to negotiate with those "on the other side." Where is this other side which you so casually dismiss? Who are the mercenaries? Who exiled them on this side? On the basis of what proof? And for how long? Who will decide when someone no longer belongs on the other side, or when someone who is now "on our side" should be sent to the other? Who has discovered this terrible conspiracy of so many Czech artists against socialism and against their fatherland just a few years after the alleged conspiracy led by the Slovak poet Laco Novomeský against socialism and the fatherland was proved to have been imagined? Who is directly responsible for compiling the aforementioned "List of Trashy Literature No. 1," and is he planning Nos. 2, 3, and so on? Who are the petty bureaucrats who ban

Brecht because of a "poor" translation, destroy copies of our classics because they object to the author's afterword, and decide that one graphic artist may make fifty prints from one plate while a more famous artist may make only thirty because he is not supposed to earn more than the former? Who determines that a famous TV actor may play only negative roles because he was a functionary of a former Union, or prevents him from working? Who gives orders to actors, artists, and musicians not to associate with their old friends who have been blacklisted, if they want to avoid a similar fate? Who violates international agreements and the Czechoslovak Constitution by secret and unlawful acts and deprives writers of their honorariums? Who permits a well-known literary scholar who was in a concentration camp during the war to be stigmatized as an enemy of the people and be replaced by an unworthy colleague who was one of the few Czechs to apply for study at German universities during the war? Who transports artists to the other side? Who gave orders to the security police to arrest writers who had legally addressed a petition to the President which contained nothing but a polite request that the authorities give clemency to political prisoners?

I would also like to speak of my own experiences. Since October 1969 I have been exposed to many discriminatory actions. Quite a few may interest you as a lawyer.

In the fall of 1969 I was expelled from the Communist Party of which I had been a member for twenty-nine years. I was not accorded the due process guaranteed by Party statutes; the objections of my cell were rejected; and I learned about my expulsion from the press . . .

In the fall of 1969 my passport was confiscated and my applications for a visa to travel abroad were either ignored or refused, with the explanation that my presence abroad would endanger national security. I was told that I could not even get an exit permit to travel in other socialist countries, though any citizen should be able to get one.

From 1969 to 1973 I was slandered on countless radio and TV shows, and even accused of having committed criminal acts. I never had the opportunity to defend myself; that I have never been interrogated proves how senseless the accusations were.

I brought a lawsuit against a newspaper in Brno which said that my father was a capitalist named Otto Hahn. My complaint was ignored, but still I had to pay for the court fees, despite the fact that it was established that my father was a Communist and his name was Ottomar Kohout.

In 1970 the Pragokoncert forbade all Czech actors to act in my plays abroad and threatened to punish those who did by preventing them from acting anywhere. Although I pay my dues to the literary fund (and have to pay it twenty times over, but I will return to this point), it has been decided by the governing body that I am not to benefit from its services.

In the summer of 1971 the Ministry of Defense deprived me of my rank as captain and demoted me to a common soldier . . .

Without legal justification secret orders have been issued to remove all of my books from bookstores and libraries. In 1970, in a second-hand shop on The Street of the 28th of October in Prague, I bought a copy of a play I had written from which my name on the book jacket and title page had been cut out with a knife.

Not a single Czech theater is allowed to stage my plays because they have received directives from high Party and government officials. The director of the Realistic Theater was issued such an order in connection with my adaptation of a Russian classic. When my play *Around the World in 80 Days* was in rehearsal, the theater in Český Tšin was forced to print new invitations, posters, and programs, from which my name was deleted. Dilia, the Prague theater and literary agency that has represented me since 1959, showed no interest in protecting me. . . .

The management of Prague theaters received instructions to exclude me from premieres by rigorously controlling the distribution of tickets. These instructions were addressed primarily to three theaters that staged more than one thousand performances in the years 1950 to 1969. I nevertheless did attend the premieres and was accused by the director of the Realistic Theater of endangering the fate of the artistic collective.

On January 1, Slovak TV broadcast my adaptation of the Soviet play *It Happened Already Long Ago* (which was premiered in 1956 in the Theater of the Czechoslovak Army), but it only credited a Slovak author with "editing." As yet, Dilia has been either unable or unwilling to seek reparations for this theft.

The director of Dilia no longer informs me about his negotiations and correspondence with foreign publishers. He aims to revoke foreign rights to my works. For two years, he has arbitrarily refused to pay me four thousand Swiss francs in compliance with my contracts. He claims that they are royalties for a banned work, though he has never read the book and refuses to show me orders he has received to stop payment. . . .

On May 13, 1972, the Ministry of Finance issued secret order No. 0266/72 to confiscate all royalties "for works published abroad which are hostile to the state and Party and whose publication and distribution have been prohibited in Czechoslovakia." This order is illegal.

I filed suit against these financial sanctions with the court in Prague 1, but as yet no legal proceedings have taken place; my urgent pleas remain unanswered, although all the legal experts have declared that the law is on my side.

In March of this year a government decree was issued (No. 20/1973) which required that authors who published abroad pay 40 percent of their royalties instead of 2 percent to the Cultural Fund; at the same time, your predecessor issued order No. 6266/73–SM4 in which he instructed the respective organs to make an exception of all authors "whose works are published in this country . . ." Therefore, I demand that the latter order be applied to me, or I will have to appeal to the courts. There is no legal basis to prevent my works from being published in this country.

Officials of two publishing companies abroad that hold world rights to my works, Eric Spiess of Bärenreiter in Kassel, and Jürgen Braunschweiger of C. J. Bucher in Lucerne, and members of their families were searched upon arrivals and departures at Prague's airport and have been forced to miss their plane several times. No proceedings have ever been taken against them, but beginning with this year, they have been unable to get entry permits. I have every reason to assume that your Ministry is responsible for this.

Many registered letters that I have sent or that have been addressed to me have mysteriously been lost. I have complained to the post office, but they are unable to do anything about it. In an envelope I sent to my Swiss publisher, a page from the *Neue Zürcher Zeitung* arrived instead of my letter.

Toward the end of last February my wife and I were committed for nine days to a special ward of the Bulovka Hospital in Prague because of suspected foot-and-mouth disease, though this disease has never occurred in Czechoslovakia. The physicians asked for our immediate release. During our stay in the hospital the police visited our weekend house near Prague without our permission. . . .

Finally, a week ago I received from the housing office an "offer" to dispose of my apartment at the Hradschiner Plaza, where I have lived for ten years, because this "apartment is needed for diplomatic purposes." When I went to the office, I was told that I was supposed to leave all the built-in facilities which were installed at my expense, including the electric stove and custom-made bookcases for five thousand books. . . .

Mr. Minister, I have cited only a few examples to make you realize how one Czech writer has been living for four years. There are dozens of similar examples, hundreds of artists and thousands of scientists, physicians, journalists, teachers, and other intellectuals far worse off than I.

I know a man who holds four university degrees but now drives a taxi; a prominent scientist who wastes away in a boarding house and has no access to a laboratory; two leading translators who make their living as nightwatchmen; three historians who repair central heating systems; a poet who, only after great effort, got employed as a bath attendant; an excellent writer who delivers milk, and another who was a porter in a hotel. When the latter gave up this position in order to write, he was told that he would lose his insurance policy. I know a man who designed world fairs but is now at home doing housework; a lifelong film director who was unemployed for two years, but when his child was dying, found employment at the post office; a critic on a Communist paper, extraordinarily educated, honest, and in poor health, who, after looking for a long time, found a job with an insurance company; two excellent literary critics, one of whom is now a window cleaner, and the other, luckier, is an usher in a theater; a popular writer who works as a cloak-room attendant in a wine cellar; another who works as a gardener; the widow of the country's greatest scriptwriter who has to care for three daughters with her earnings as a cleaning lady because she, too, was discriminated against by Dilia. One of her daughters had to leave the journalism department of the university. The other won a national literary competition for young talent, but despite this prize, top examination scores, and the support of all her professors, she has already been rejected twice by the Film Academy. My extremely gifted friends—former students, professors, journalists, and political scientists—are employed by the dozens as bricklayers, drivers, salesmen, and steam-shovel operators. Since my youth I have known a very gifted scientist who was chairman of the Party organization at the Institute for Atomic Research. They wore him down to such a degree that he was in a psychiatric clinic for two years; in March of this year he hanged himself. In writing this letter I keep this friend uppermost in my mind.

Despite these conditions, your predecessor dared to say on TV that "the situation in the field of culture is normal."

Actually things are very abnormal and have been so for five years. And there seems to be no way out in sight. Your inaugural address certainly did not suggest one. Yet how is this situation possible? What do you hope to achieve? Why should brilliant minds go to waste, especially when we are now exposed to all the dangers of consumer society? Why should gifted people and their families who have committed no crime be arrested in their own country? We have seen how, after killing each other for years, the parties in Vietnam became unified. Now we are seeing the statesmen of two great powers divided by the ocean, language, ideology, and ways of life, reaching out their hands in cooperation. Is it impossible for us to become a unified nation because we have different views on what socialism should be?

Our society tries to rehabilitate even those who were sentenced for crimes. Yet why does it ban many of the intelligentsia whose only "crime" is that they hold views that only the future will prove right or wrong? After five years don't we have the right to ask how long this ban will last?

We expect help only from our homeland and the community of socialist states. If we expected help from the outside, we would go to America, Switzerland, or Germany, the countries where our books are published and our plays performed. Nobody believes that the rest of the world will help us if we are imprisoned, or that it will feed us if our income is taken away. Therefore, few of us go into exile. I myself remain in Czechoslovakia because I am not accustomed to knocking at the door and then running away, because even under horrible conditions I want to participate in the development of Czech culture; because I know that this society, if it wants to live without shame, will understand my behavior and respect my civil rights.

It would be unrealistic to expect that we will immediately be permitted free discussions on TV or in newspapers. But why not stop the raiding of our libraries? Why can't those books discussed in textbooks be published again? Why can't we publish works of authors who have deeply explored our human fate? Why can't real literary critics be allowed to work? Why can't all those who have proved by their silence that they have a lot to say begin to sing, make films, perform, and exhibit their works? As for myself, why can't my new piece about Leonid Andrejew be produced in Prague instead of in Düsseldorf, where it premiered? Why couldn't I be permitted to direct, at least abroad, plays that are often produced in socialist countries? Why can't the state of emergency, which is as anachronistic as the Cold War, be ended?

Only a cynic would believe it possible to nurture a new generation of artists with stipends, prizes, and travels abroad. Serious works can be expected only from people who see with their own eyes what has happened to their precursors.

For a long time I thought that Karel Čapek would be the last of the hounded, that the textbooks of tomorrow would not be collections of material banned in the past, and that the new society, which enlightened men and women helped to create, would never permit its artists to suffer injustice. I was wrong.

Twenty-three years ago you and I traveled together from Moscow to Prague. You carried diplomatic papers; I was already a writer. I think I will remain a writer even when the future finds you playing a different role. For you, your present activity

in the realm of culture is a job. For me, it is my destiny. This
is why I am writing this letter, at a time when the Conference
on Security and Cooperation—a result of the efforts of progressive people all over the world—is about to convene. I conclude
by saying that the attitude of the statesmen at this Conference
should be that "the cooperation and security of Europe can be
established only when security and cooperation is established
within individual states themselves."

PAVEL KOHOUT, writer
Prague
June 1973

Alexander Dubček to the Federal Parliament of Czechoslovakia and the Slovak National Council

I am writing this letter for one reason: to alert the public to the fact that our legislative system, and Czechoslovak democracy in general, is being crippled from within. In a totalitarian system, the abuse of political office, either by individuals or groups, can easily develop and thus undermine the democratic structure of the Party and the republic. In our society, abuses have been many and varied, and the end result has been the abolition of majority rule.

As the influence of the military on our government has grown, the potential for the abuse of power by government officials has become unlimited. This is particularly true of the Ministry of the Interior, which now views itself as capable of operating above the law. The "spider web" of power and influence woven by such agencies extends to our courts and prosecutors, who have lost their independence. Our judicial system is nothing more than a slave to the Ministry of Interior and its organs. And without an independent legal system it is pointless to speak of justice in our country. The real tragedy is that all this has taken place in a socialist society.

My assertions, I believe, are completely justified. In previous letters—the last was dated March 1973—I gave vivid examples of how my personal freedom has been violated, and I shall take this opportunity to cite additional incidents that support my allegations and prove that branches of the Ministry of Internal Affairs and State Security have acted illegally. In doing so

I want to stress that I am not writing simply for my own benefit but also for the sake of all of my fellow countrymen whose lives are entangled in the invisible and horrible "web," and who suffer pain and disgrace because of it.

In order to describe in detail what has been happening to me, I have decided to focus on only a few incidents. There are others, but to write about them in the way I want to would require much more space.

Once or twice a month my wife receives a visit from a woman. This woman is fifty years old and has three children; she is not a member of the Party. August 18 is her birthday, and because we had never been to her home, we promised to visit her on this occasion.

My wife and I and our son left our home at eight o'clock in the evening and decided to visit my brother-in-law on Mudron Street on our way to the woman's house. I told my son to wait for us in the car on a parallel street while we went in for a brief visit. During the twenty minutes we spent with my wife's brother, my son noticed that two manned police cars were parked nearby.

After this visit my son drove us to the woman's apartment in the center of Bratislava and then went home. (My wife worries when no one is at home for too long.) When we came to the side entrance of the building, we stopped for a while and watched a man go in. When he saw us he stopped first in front of one apartment door and then in front of another, acting as if he were looking for his residence. At ten o'clock, when our friends escorted us to the main entrance, we saw the same man enter the building a second time. It became obvious to us that he wanted to find out which apartment belonged to our hostess.

Once again on the street, I studied the neighborhood carefully. As we approached a corner I noticed a man in a yellow vest who stopped before another man who held a briefcase. The man in the yellow vest waited until we crossed the intersection. To make sure that we were not being followed, my wife and I took a trolley heading in the opposite direction from our home. We soon got off, and so did the man in the yellow vest. Quickly we crossed the platform and prepared to board another trolley now heading in the direction of our home. The man in the yellow vest tried to slip unobtrusively into the same car, but just before we climbed aboard, I stopped and asked him what time it was. He was stunned, and it took him a few moments to regain enough composure to answer me.

We arrived home in about ten minutes. The evening's events gave my wife a severe headache, which kept her awake most of the night. Thus I did not tell her that that same night, as I walked our sheepdog in front of our house, I saw two men patrolling the street. Twice I left the dog in front of the house and tried to approach them. Each time, they kept a distance of 25 to 30 meters.

On August 21, accompanied by one of my colleagues, I drove my Land Rover to the forestry plant in Sastin-Straze. As we began the journey I noticed two cars, Russian Volgas, that seemed to be following us, but I was not sure at first, for at times they hid behind other cars. Somewhat suspicious, I decided not to take the main route to Sastin-Straze behind the village of Malachy but instead took the Brno Road in order to return to the crossroads through an open field. I assumed that the State Security Police would follow me, and I picked a suitable place to wait for them.

I did not have to wait long. Convinced that they were fulfilling their duty in exemplary fashion, I continued my journey; and in spite of the rugged terrain and the dusty, bumpy roads I had taken, they were still in pursuit. As we left the field, I assured my colleague that I had not been mistaken, for the rear-view mirror had shown me what he could not see.

At the plant, some of my co-workers and I discussed the competitiveness among the drivers, and then we went to the wood shack. We reset the power saws and checked the condition of some of the other machinery. The open fields around us allowed us, while we worked, to see the gray Volga waiting in the shadow of a truck parked near the station and the second car guarding the station's entrance. When we finished our inspection, one of the workers gave us a tour of the grounds and showed us where private recreation houses were being built. My fellow workers from Sastin-Straze noticed my "guardians," and one of them asked in a trembling voice, "Is this the way they watch you?"

A storm was in the making all day, and we decided to work without stopping for lunch in order to finish before it broke. When our work was finally completed, another of my co-workers offered to take us to his home for some bacon and sausage. There is no need to tell you how gladly I accepted this modest but sincere offer.

During the fifth and sixth of December, I substituted for the man who was to drive to the Duchinka branch of the plant in Topolcany. My co-workers there were experimenting with new methods adapted to local conditions. A few old buildings still exist near the main plant, and as I explored the yard I heard the ringing sound of a sledgehammer coming apparently from an old barn. I entered the barn and peered through the smoke at a blacksmith who was working there. I asked him how he was doing and began to look around the forge.

The blacksmith was an old man, worn out but powerfully built. He stared at me for a while, and I became conscious of my forestry uniform which I wear occasionally in the winter but never in the summer. Then he said, "I think I've seen you somewhere before; I just can't remember where."

"It's possible," I replied. "We're almost neighbors. I'm from nearby, from Uhrovce."

He thought for a while, studying me, and then said with a shy smile, "I know. You are Mr. Dubček."

He seemed embarrassed at knowing who I was, but I moved closer to him and said, "If you don't have anything in the fire, I'd like to try to make a horseshoe."

"Are you sure you know how?"

"I'm not sure," I said. "I worked at the forge in the Skodka factory for a few years some time ago, and I knew how to then. Originally, I was a metal worker and I have experience. If you don't mind, I'd like to try."

The smith was pleased and encouraged me.

"Why not?," he said. "I have a number of old pieces of iron you can use, or if you want a new one, help yourself. They're laid out according to size."

"No," I said. "I don't want any of them; they're mass-produced. I'd prefer a traditional one, made from a single piece. That's how I used to do it."

With the eye of an expert, he picked a suitable piece from a heap of old iron, took it in his hand and judged its weight and strength. Then he started the forge.

"How shall we do it?" he asked.

"You are the master and I am your apprentice," I answered, easing the tension with a joke.

"Then take the hammer."

I did this with a feeling of satisfaction, and soon the barn echoed with the familiar sound of hammers striking metal in unison.

When he put the finished shoe in the fire the second time, the smith remarked, "I knew you could do it from the start. The way you stood at the anvil, grasping the handle of the hammer first with your left hand, putting the head under your arm and then holding it with your right . . ."

Writing these words now brings back that feeling of deep satisfaction I then felt. It was seldom that I had the opportunity to go to forestry workshops—now, of course, I am forbidden to go anywhere—and I can remember looking through a small window in the shop and seeing snow falling in soft, white flakes . . .

Perhaps because he was pleased with his "apprentice," or maybe because he simply had enjoyed the work, he said in a humble voice when we were finished, "Let's make another one, which will be mine."

I readily agreed, but then one of the technicians from the forestry commission came to tell me that I had to leave, and the shoe was never made.

I stayed a while longer, helping him repair a blunt pickax. We also played that game of holding the hammer with only two fingers, and I was the winner. Finally, while the technician and another man waited impatiently, we said good-bye and shared a long, firm handshake. I drove home to Bratislava through Topolcany on roads covered with glittering snow.

I must apologize for being so long-winded and detailed about the incident with the blacksmith. Perhaps it is because of the long hours of interrogation by the security branch of the Ministry of Interior that I endured. They made a terrible fuss about it, and the commotion spread through every branch of the forestry division—from the smith himself, all the way to the heads of the county.

Many wondered what kind of crime I had committed to cause such a stir. They wouldn't believe that what I have just told you was the whole truth, assuming, of course, that no heretical meeting took place. I was more puzzled than anyone. My companions on the trip must have told the truth, yet the chairman of the Party and his colleagues received a rushed report from the interrogating officers that I had tried to gain popularity in Topolcany, and did so by making monogrammed horseshoes and giving them away . . .

What I have told you here are the facts of the case. I don't know if I will ever see the kind blacksmith from that remote village again, but I can imagine how he must feel. As a man who thought of his life and work in simple terms, he could not possibly comprehend the "spider web" in which he suddenly found himself entangled, or be aware of those who have woven this web and the vast network of invisible threads that it is.

On January 31, I reversed roles and began pursuing my pursuers. I began to study them, and I learned that they no longer wear the leather overcoats and jackets they wore in the past, or the turned-up collars from the old movies, or the stiff hats like those worn by secret agent Brettschneider in Hasek's *Svejk*. These days they wear regular suits and look like ordinary citizens. Still, you can pick them out of a crowd if you know they are following you.

On the aforementioned day things were quite simple: a passenger on the bus I was riding home got off at the same station as I did and then fell in line with passengers who were waiting for the bus to make the return trip. Now this is certainly not the way a normal man travels, and I was quite suspicious. Halfway to the crosswalk I turned around, walked up to the man and asked him the time. His response to this simple question was strange: He acted as if I had slapped him, and it took him some time before he recovered sufficiently to figure out which hand his watch was on. Pleased with my work for that day, I went straight home. I didn't even look back to see if I was still being followed.

May 4, 1974: Around nine o'clock in the morning I joined

a friend for a drive in his car. He had a Simca, and I wanted him
to help me determine how reliable my knowledge of my pursuers was.

After we had been on the road for a while I gave him a
description of what I thought the pursuit car looked like—a
Skodka, Identification No. PF-125—and told him to watch for it.
Then I began to drive really fast. We passed through the town
of Modra, and through Pezinok, and still the Skodka followed
closely. Finally, I had to slow down—God forbid that they may
have thought that I was trying to flee the country by driving
south of the Carpathian mountains and into neutral Austria. My
friend found out that I was right.

(I apologize for my care-free tone here, but I can't help
taking these things lightly. My tone is essential to my survival
in this social and civil war that has been waged against me for
so many years.)

On August 10, 1974, I did a lot of traveling. First, I drove
to Topolcany to congratulate my Aunt Zuzka on her birthday, and from there to Uhrovce to visit the graves of my
parents, founding members of the Communist Party of Czechoslovakia, and of my brother, who died in the Slovak national upheaval against the Nazis. Then I went to Trencin to
visit my brother-in-law's family; he and his wife were cele-
brating their fiftieth anniversary. My pursuers had been with
me ever since Bratislava.

During all of this it surprised me that neither my wife nor
my friend, whom we had picked up at the hospital, noticed
anything. At one point my friend said to me, "You see, nobody
bothers you; you are free to visit your relatives undisturbed.

"When I called you on the phone to ask you if you were
going to Trencin and if you could take me along, you said there
might be some problems. I thought you were trying to tell me
that you didn't want me along . . ." Then, jokingly, he added:
"Nothing can happen to me. They call me a doctor but force me
to work in a warehouse. I wanted to make some money feeding
cows and pigs. First I was promised the job, but in the end I
never got it."

An hour passed, and then I said to him, "You should know
why I didn't want you to come with us; now I will show you

something, namely how the spider web has trapped us, even though, at first, the threads are hardly noticeable.

"There are two cars, one in front and the other behind us. They are driven by members of the State Security Police. They have been following us since we left Bratislava."

My friend looked at me in bewilderment; he hadn't noticed anything. I pointed out to him the two cars and then began to drive in a way that convinced him that I was telling the truth. By the time we had driven some distance from Hlohovec, heading toward Topolcany, and had passed a number of villages and crossroads, both my friend and my wife no longer doubted that what I had told them about the cars was true.

Just to prove my point, I stopped the car on a curve behind a hill. The driver of the car behind me, a Fiat (Identification No. BAD-9381), was not expecting this and passed me. I began to follow him at a speed of about forty m.p.h. and he reduced his speed to match mine, though there were no other cars in front of him. When I increased my speed to sixty-five, so did he. I told my wife that the other car would be waiting for us somewhere up ahead.

We stopped at a cornfield to rest, and then continued our journey. At Luzany, the next village, my "guardians" were waiting for me near a small diner to the left of the road that led into the town. I saw one of the men in the Fiat leave the car and head for the diner, while his partner remained in the car. Just as he was about to go inside, I got out, walked over to the Fiat, opened the door, and asked the man in the car how late it was.

The other man didn't bother to buy anything. He ran over to me and began shouting at me in the manner of someone who is conscious of his own power. I asked him why he was so upset, since I had done nothing wrong by asking politely about the time.

"You have no business in my car!" he yelled.

By that time I couldn't control myself any longer and shouted back, "This is not your car!"

He stared at me with a look full of hatred, and I had the feeling that if he had had the power, he would have killed me on the spot. I closed the door, went back to my car, and drove off to visit my Aunt Zuzka on her seventy-sixth birthday.

On another occasion I stopped in Bratislava at the bank at Stara Vajnorska to pay by check for some bricks for my fireplace. Somehow, I had lost my pursuers for a short time. I imagine they were running around like madmen trying to find me, and a young boy who had seen the back of my Simca behind a wooden partition at the local transportation plant couldn't hide his pleasure. . . . I was not surprised when my wife told me later that a commission from Bratislava had checked to see whether I had obtained permission to build the fireplace from the proper authorities in the city. No doubt they were surprised to find that everything was in order. . . .

I am pleased to hear that the Party leadership has been publicly demanding freedom for Chile and for the Secretary General, Corvalan, on such occasions as the May Day celebration, the anniversary of the Slovak upheaval against the Nazis, and Thanksgiving. Yet I am troubled by the discrepancy between such statements and the events and practices I have described. Everything I have told you has happened in a socialist state under the leadership of the Communist Party and has affected the lives of other Communists, internationalists, and Czechoslovak patriots!

Were I the only one harassed, I would not be writing this letter. But intimidation has become the norm in our political system. The fact of the matter is that methods which did much to harm socialism in the past and which have since been condemned by hundreds of thousands of Communists, indeed, by the entire Communist movement, are now being used and even encouraged.

The period after the events of August 1968 (*i.e.*, the occupation of Czechoslovakia by Soviet armies) has been characterized by the gradual elimination of all reforms by partisan groups that claim they are fighting a counterrevolutionary movement. The consequence has been fear, which is felt not only by former Party functionaries and members of the government, but also by women's groups, trade unions, associations of anti-fascist fighters, cultural and art groups, and other organizations of the National Front. Moreover, the official policy of the new Party leadership threatens the very existence of these organizations and deprives their members of their rights as citizens.

Officially, these practices are said to reflect the *leading role of the Party* and *the revival of its influence* in the society. I underline these words because it was already recognized at the meeting of the Central Committee that the Party, because it had violated the Leninist principles of Party unity, had lost its influence and slipped into a deep crisis. The present policy of the Party can be easily justified by appealing to this recognition.

[Dubček then goes on to describe the effect of statements he previously had made to different institutions. In his letters he made them aware of the violations of his personal freedom and of the law in general. On May 31 and June 26, 1970, he sent a protest to the Secretary General of the Communist Party of Czechoslovakia (CPC), Dr. Gustáv Husák. Husák answered many months later, stating that everything had been investigated and that it had been determined that the Ministry of the Interior had not acted illegally in his case, either then or in the past. On October 8, 1970, Dubček wrote to the Minister of the Interior of the Czechoslovak Republic himself; he never received a reply. On January 6, 1973, Dubček filed a complaint with the General Prosecutor. Again, he received no reply.]

On June 14 I was requested to appear before the Ministry of the Interior of the Slovak Socialist Republic. At that meeting, three hours were spent trying to persuade me to sign a statement acknowledging that all the incidents I had described in my letter to the General Prosecutor were untrue and that consequently my complaint was unfounded. I of course refused to sign the statement. That was the net effect of my letter to the General Prosecutor, and, as you can see from this one, the Ministry has made no attempt to change or correct its behavior. In fact, precisely the opposite has happened: I am under more intensive surveillance than ever before.

Neither the organs of the Ministry of the Interior nor those of the Party have any reason to harass me. I work as an employee of the Forestry Department, in the Engineering Section, and devote the rest of my time to my family. Still, I have been explosed to unstinting social and psychological harassment during the past year. This situation has made work extremely difficult for me; in addition, my sins are considered hereditary, and surveillance is extended to my whole family.

As in my former complaints, I wish to make a moral accusation against the present regime in this letter, and present unequivocal proof of the abuse of power in our society.

There are forces in some branches of the State Security Service that want the power to control the entire political and social life of our country. These forces feel entitled to interfere with Party matters and use, or rather, abuse their power and positions by carrying out the illegal activities I have mentioned. A spider web is being woven in the form of a network of undercover agents, who operate not only in my immediate environment but also in the whole society. As a result, the socialist cause is being discredited.

Corruption grows in a party or system where there is no opportunity for open discussions and no provisions for checking the activity of the higher organs. In our system, the fear of suffering hardship or of losing one's life motivates many citizens to accept decisions they do not agree with. This hypocrisy flourishes: One speaks at meetings differently from the way one does in the privacy of one's home or in the company of friends. In the Party organizations, trade unions, youth and women's groups, and other organizations of the National Front, it has become all but impossible to defend one's own convictions. People are therefore becoming indifferent, and an atmosphere of distrust and fear pervades. Under such conditions, it is impossible for a democratic majority to rule the Party.

We have experienced enough to know that Marxism-Leninism is not a stiff dogma; it does not provide the same formulas for all Communist parties, regardless of their stage of development. The works of Marx and Lenin are informed by general principles that are to be used by a Party only as guidelines for a specific socioeconomic program. Thus, I refuse to be lumped with traitors of the Party simply because like many others, I have different but equally valid views concerning Party policy at this stage of development. I should not be condemned for offering alternative solutions to the problems and difficulties our nation is facing.

Moreover, the position that Party policy should be followed blindly is unacceptable in a socialist society. Just as reprehensible is the notion that it should be enforced by armed government agencies or by the armed forces of other countries, as was the case in 1968.

Here, I want to repeat something that I stated in my letter to the Central Committee of the CPC: The way out of the political crisis which began in the fifties was in sight once the Party and the government adapted new positions. However, with the occupation of our nation by the Soviet armies in August 1968, the crisis deepened. Now the way out cannot be found in the "lessons" that are being taught by the new government. The solution lies only in applying the resolutions of the plenary sessions of the Central Committee of November 1968.

At the plenary session held in the fall of 1969, the Praesidium of the Party presented a resolution that voided the November one. At that time I openly declared that we were inviting the destruction of the Party and society. It was for this reason that I and others were accused of "treason against the Party, the working class, and the people." According to the new leadership, I had endangered not only socialism but also our alliances and the unification of our society. Yet I am convinced that the November resolution accepted after the military intervention of August 1968 would have been instrumental in creating political unity within the Party and the state, for it criticized not only right-wing opportunism but also sectarianism, which the new leadership has invited. Enlisting the aid of dogmatic factions and pretending to fight against "right-wing opportunism" and "counterrevolution," it has annulled the November resolution, which was designed as a basis for unity under the conditions brought about by the Soviet occupation. Thus, the present regime split the Party.

What may our younger generation learn from this? What may the parties of Yugoslavia, Italy, France, Spain, Sweden, Belgium, and Finland learn from the Warsaw Pact countries, whose armies—with the exception of Rumania's—were sent to interfere with the internal affairs of our country? Part of the "lesson" is that during the critical and tragic days of August

1968, the organs of State Security did not arrest a single counter-revolutionary, though they knew exactly where most government, Parliament, and Czech National Council officials could be found.

According to the announcement of the official Soviet press agency, the armies of the Warsaw Pact countries entered Czechoslovakia at the invitation of a group of Czechoslovak representatives. This group had no legitimacy, and if the invitation was sent at all, it was sent by an extremist faction. The consequences of their action is an offense and a humiliation, a moral and ideological degradation of the entire Communist Party of Czechoslovakia and our two nations.

Yes, they humiliated and offended the Party, and the Czech and Slovak nations. They harmed the entire Communist and socialist movement in our country, whether they intended to or not. They damaged the relationship between Czechoslovakia and the Soviet Union, disregarding our history of cooperation and the gratitude we owe the Red Army for liberating our country from the Nazis. Moreover, it is regrettable that many founding members of the Party, supporters of Czechoslovak-Soviet friendship, and young Communists who participated in the anti-fascist and nationalist fights for freedom, are being dragged through the mud, so to speak. Many workers who have made incredible sacrifices to build a socialist state and who have proved their allegiance to the Party and the Soviet Union, have suddenly been declared "anti-Soviet" and have been hurt, morally, socially, and materially. Important moral and ideological values have been denigrated, and creativity in the fields of art and culture, and particularly among the working class, is on the wane. And all of this has happened in a socialist state that has sacrificed many lives to come into being.

The fact of the matter is that we have been punished for the actions we staged in January 1968 and for the principles that informed them, by the advocates of a dogmatic approach to the building of a socialist society, and by the adherents of a system of personal power that suppresses the democratic elements of Marxism-Leninism. There are no "lessons" to be learned here. The lessons that the present Party leadership formulated as a political platform are not part of the solution of the crisis faced by our Party and society, and do not lead to the development of a better sociopolitical system. The platform that presently defines the nation's political course is causing moral, ideological, and cultural stagnation. In choosing between the two courses charted in 1968 and 1969, there can be no compromise; they are mutually exclusive.

While the present state of affairs prevails, our people will continue to resist it, for it was not brought about, as the leadership falsely claims, by democratic means but by absolutist exercises of power.

The crucial difference, thus, between the Party's current policy and the one developed in 1968 is that the latter was based on democratic principles and the former on an inflexible ideology. In January of 1968 we tried to foster progressive socialism. We tried to free socialism from the anachronistic deformities and one-sidedness of Marxism. This one-sidedness is now the basis for present policy, which emphasizes only one aspect of Marxism at the expense of all others.

[Dubček adds that it is not important whether his thesis is accepted or not. What is important is that "sooner or later, either step by step or in some other fashion, the contradictions of the present crisis will be solved." This is as necessary to Czechoslovakia's development as cooperation with nonsocialist countries, although until quite recently they were regarded as an impassive, hostile, imperialist force.]

The peaceful coexistence of all nations is highly desirable and will benefit the socialist cause. Therefore, to denounce the Party leadership of 1968 as "revisionist" because they believed in peaceful coexistence is unjustified. "Revisionist" is a label used to induce fear and has the same effect as the church's calling someone a "heretic."

My historical perspective leads me to refute the statements and conclusions of the present Party leadership. They are wrong when they say that we revised Lenin's theory of the Party, for in 1968 Lenin's principles were operative in the Party system. Had this not been true, we could hardly have spoken of a new type of Communist Party. Since the new Party leadership came to power in 1969, the most important principle for the creative development of the Party—the inclusion of the working class and of all citizens in the planning and realization of government and Party policy—has been suppressed or ignored.

The fact that both now and in the past the Party leadership has tried to build a socialist state without the cooperation of most Party members, workers, trade unions, and organizations of women, students, and youth is the cause of the present crisis. The Party will be strong only when its leaders realize that they must make sure of eyes other than their own; they must regard Party members not as the blind masses who require spoon-feeding and strong leadership. Similarly, lack of approval for the new, developing political line must not be viewed, a priori, as "hostile, anti-Party behavior." Even less permissible should be the current practice of actually punishing Party dissidents by jeopardizing their social and material well-being. This is an abuse of power that can only weaken the Party and destroy our Socialist society.

[Unequivocally, Dubček protests accusations made against the old Party leadership and argues that the charges of the present regime that "after January 1968 a retreat to capitalism was attempted" are unfounded. He explains that what occurred at that time was merely an attempt to effect economic reforms that had been planned earlier. These reforms were designed to introduce in the factories greater material rewards for everyone who took an interest in the development of the economy. The reforms were not oriented against planning, as it is now claimed, but against controlling the factories "from above." Regarding socialist agriculture, Dubček further states that "in not a single case has the collective form of production been abandoned; attempts were never made."]

One of the most incredible accusations made by the present regime is that we planned to isolate our country from the international Communist community. This professed concern justified "renewed" cooperation with the Soviet Union and the other countries of the socialist bloc. Such cooperation has much to recommend it, but it need not be forced down the nation's throat. The issue is raised at every level of Party involvement, even if unrelated topics such as essential services, productivity, or technical development are being discussed. This propaganda is counterproductive, which must be painfully obvious to all concerned. But dogmatism has become so prevalent that no one dares to object for fear that he will immediately be accused of being an enemy of the Soviet Union.

Such demagoguery will certainly discredit the idea of international cooperation. The denunciation of many Communist revolutionaries, resistance fighters, and contributors to the socialist cause as "anti-Soviet elements" is increasingly giving rise to anti-Soviet sentiment.

To prove my point, I could give a full list of famous revolutionaries, artists, musicians, and members of the Academy who have all been silenced. I could speak of thousands, indeed hundreds of thousands, of Communists and non-Communists, who fought shoulder to shoulder with Soviet soldiers for the liberation of Czechoslovakia and the building of a socialist state, all of whom are now stigmatized as anti-Soviet.

Half a million alleged anti-Soviet members of the Party have been expelled; many were well-known community and national figures. And what consequences, other than the emergence of anti-Sovietism among the rest of the members of the Party and the public, can be expected when citizens are being labeled as "enemies" for no apparent reason? These defamations and the new and more violent methods for achieving work quotas—methods that are already acknowledged as obsolete and have been publicly denounced as aberrations—suggest that it is the new Party leadership that promotes anti-Sovietism in Czechoslovakia.

I have always known, as did most of the representatives of the previous government, that Czechoslovakia cannot follow a policy of isolation from the Soviet Union; in fact, cooperation is essential to our development. This was, and will remain, the basis of Czechoslovakia's foreign policy. Therefore, I cannot state strongly enough how false are the accusations against our "anti-Soviet" policies and against our alleged attempts to separate our nation from the socialist community. My comrades and

I worked hard simply to develop a short-term program for the National Front and to make it a reality. The issue was never revisionism but rather, wider cooperation between nations and the right of each national Party and state to govern its internal affairs according to the needs and will of the people.

It is true that in our Action Program we stated the necessity of supporting all progressive and anti-fascist forces even if they were not Communist. But it is not true that we looked first to the Social Democrats and Willy Brandt for a new direction. We wished also to promote cooperation between non-Communist and leftist parties throughout the world. The activities of the Communist parties in Italy, Spain, France, and elsewhere, the legalization of the Communist Party in the Federal Republic of Germany, and the oppression of socialists in Chile taught us the importance of that goal.

What is the criteria that decides whether someone is permitted to remain a member of the Party or proves that he is a good Marxist-Leninist? At present, it seems that Party membership is determined by whether or not one agrees with the policy of those who welcomed the invasion of Czechoslovakia by the five nations of the Warsaw Pact; declares that the Prague Spring was opportunist and revisionist; approves the expulsion of the "revisionist" and "opportunist" leadership of the Party under Alexander Dubček; and agrees with the new Marxist-Leninist doctrine.

Apparently, everyone who says he is a "Marxist-Leninist" is automatically one, while those who oppose the present regime are opportunists acting against the interests of the Party. However, the violent and methodical expulsion of many qualified people from the Party because they held opinions that departed from the established line has been harmful to our country. The intelligentsia have borne the brunt of the repression. Those who could have contributed much to the development of our society by their thoughts and their writings have been silenced, in spite of the fact that we know from past experience how helpful their work has been to the socialist cause.

In my opinion, the leading role of the working class in the struggle for socialism has diminished, for the working class is increasingly being manipulated by those who are running the country. What the working class had considered progressive has been taken away from them, and another platform has been forced on them. Their influence in public affairs, insofar as it exists at all, has been minimized; and what is far worse, to my mind, the people no longer have the right to express without fear their views on Party policy.

The current program of the Party may have disastrous effects. It could weaken the influence of the Communist Party after the triumph of the proletariat and cut down on voluntary participation in the revolution and in the building of socialism.

[Dubček then refers to the mechanistic comparisons of Czechoslovakia in 1968 and Hungary in 1956, and finds them false. He believes that it is crucial for us to see the differences between the two crises. In Czechoslovakia the Party was on the way to solving acute problems by democratic means. A new Party and state leadership developed in a democratic way, and did not feel threatened by the masses. The solution of immediate problems was formulated in the Action Program, which the masses understood and supported. As the working spirit of cooperation grew, the army, the security forces, and the People's Militia backed the political program of the Party's Central Committee, and represented a force that would have made it impossible to overthrow socialism.]

. . . An awareness of the differences and particularities of the socialist revolution in each country must play an important part in the formulation of domestic policy and in the relationship among Communist, socialist, and workers' parties. If these issues are overlooked, great harm can come to the movements for Communist, socialist, and national liberation.

For instance, should we teach our Polish comrades how to go about collectivizing farmland—something we achieved long ago—or should we deduce from the fact that they have not yet solved the problem that they are attempting to conserve the private ownership of land and maintain capitalism? Neither would be correct; only our Polish comrades know best when and how to solve this problem. Yet, the leadership of the United Polish Workers' Party tried to force us to take senseless actions in 1968, even though in Poland universities were closed, the teacher associations had been dissolved, the dissatisfaction of the people had reached a high point, and such tragedies like the shooting of workers were taking place. Did the former Party leadership of Poland think that they could solve their problems by crusading against Czechoslovakia's leaders and their policies?

There is no clearer proof of the violation of national sovereignty than the position some Communist parties have taken against the Union of Yugoslavian Communists; some have argued that Yugoslavia is not even a socialist country. This is very difficult to believe, for anyone can see that despite the strong pressure we brought to bear on that country, our Yugoslavian comrades resisted and passed the difficult test of building a socialist society in a country that is isolated from the rest of the socialist world.

Furthermore, what would our comrades from the German Democratic Republic say if we compared them to ourselves and criticized them for permitting small-scale private industry and other private enterprises on a rather widespread basis because we thought this practice would lead to a revival of capitalism? Certainly it is their right to determine the most successful and effective approaches to their own problems. Yet the former Party leadership of the G.D.R. pressured us and wanted to prescribe the course of action we should take, and even went so far as to outline our policy vis-à-vis Willy Brandt, when we had not yet even formulated our own.

The mere mention that we intended to get a loan from a developed country was declared dangerous by our "allies" because of the possibility of increased dependence on capitalism. This is nonsense. Any economist knows that such loans would have been used for technological improvements that would have benefited the whole nation. Today, not only are such credits taken for granted but even capitalist banks are permitted to operate in socialist countries. As a marginal note it should be remembered that once we accept the principle of peaceful coexistence between countries with different sociopolitical systems, it follows that economic and technological cooperation and trade between these countries will take place.

If a good, solid relationship among Communist nations exists, none should find the principle of national sovereignty threatening. This principle should be the topic of discussion at an international forum of the Communist parties of Europe, or even of all the nations of the world. The declaration made by the Soviet government in 1956—that no Communist Party has the right to support the activities of factions in other parties— could be accepted as a point of departure.

Respect for this principle would have hampered the activities of those individuals and groups with views different from those of the Central Committee of the CPC who, in 1968— according to the official statement of the Soviet press agency concerning the military occupation of Czechoslovakia by some of the Warsaw Pact countries—encouraged the Soviet intervention. This group took upon itself great responsibility without the consent of many Czechoslovaks. Although they espouse Leninism today, at that time they abandoned the Leninist principle of majority rule and used methods that had never been used before in the Communist movement. They arranged the arrest of leading government representatives by masked members of the State Security Agency and revoked the policy that had been approved by the nation, thus taking advantage of a situation they had created to force their own ideas upon the country. Yet they claim that their views are Marxist and universal (if Lenin could only rise from the dead to see what is being sanctioned in his name!), and proclaim to the world that they have remained faithful to the Warsaw Pact.

This is simple demagoguery. Did the former leadership of our Party or the government at any time question the Pact or attempt to violate it? The Warsaw Pact was necessary for the collective defense of each signatory if attacked. Our attitude toward the obligations of the agreement is, like that of the other members, including Rumania, stated in public documents. We never failed to meet these obligations. It was clear in 1968—and it is even clearer today—that the existence of two opposing military camps in a single country represents a great obstacle to human progress.

In addition to protesting the actions of the Ministry of the Interior, I am also stating some of my own views. Under present conditions I have neither the opportunity nor the desire to speak directly with anyone about these matters. I have written everything at one time, and I am aware that some of my ideas need refinement. However, my concern is not merely with clarity of expression. I want this letter to stand as a testament to the times in which it was written.

The fact is that our system is inconsistent with the tenets of Marxism-Leninism. It must be overthrown. My quarrel is not only with those individuals who, while claiming to defend the Marxist cause, have perpetuated tyranny. The very philosophy of this kind of government, which rests on the manipulation of the masses, unquestioned obedience, and strict discipline (all for the protection of socialism, of course), must be shown for what it is.

Unless we expose this system, our younger generation will come to accept injustice as a way of life and become indifferent to basic human rights. Fighting for these rights is justifiable even under socialism. The Party should be a strong promoter of them.

I am stating my political views and convictions in this letter in order to show you that I am not a "case" for the Security Service. What I have written here is not "political agitation." Neither are my accounts of conversations with my co-workers and relatives nor those held at the graves of my parents and brother in Uhrovce, as my "guards" imagined when they drew their web around me. If you want to know my views and opinions, here they are; I have done you the favor of writing them down.

One might say that I (and I am not alone) am "guilty" because my evaluation of our nation's development is different from that of the regime. Yet I maintain that my concern is still with solving our deepening and seemingly permanent crisis, and I strongly protest the injustices that I and others are subjected to for making our views known. Are we under permanent surveillance to ensure that the secret police will have work? Or should we consider ourselves fortunate that we receive the same attention as the President, who, it is well known, must place two transistor radios on his window during certain conversations?

Finally, I want to comment on the choice of the code word, "briza" (birch tree), used by that group in the Ministry of the Interior that keeps such a careful "watch" over me. This word seems to function as camouflage: It would have been too obvious to use the word "dub" (oak), or even "dubček" (little oak). "Briza" is a good choice, however, as the birch is not a strong tree, but it endures even in the most trying circumstance.

A spider web of suspicion, guilt, and fear has entangled our nation. Those who spin this web abuse their power and violate Party and socialist principles. Even worse, they violate human rights.

ALEXANDER DUBČEK
Bratislava
October 28, 1974

Dr. František Kriegel, Dr. Gertruda Sekaninová-Čakrtová, and František Vodsloň to the Federal Parliament of Czechoslovakia

On August 1, 1975, the representatives of thirty-five nations gathered for the Helsinki Conference and signed the Final Act on Security and Cooperation. This document supports many of the principles that progressive movements throughout Europe have been fighting for. Among other things, it states that it is the duty and right of every country to defend its sovereignty, that national values should be passed from generation to generation, and that the working class has always tried to secure political and civil rights. The pronouncements having to do with national sovereignty and peaceful coexistence are especially important to Czechoslovakia.

As is the case with any agreement, the value of the Final Act on Security and Cooperation depends on whether the signatories respect its provisions. Three months have passed, and still we see no sign that the Czechoslovak government will comply with the agreement. We therefore submit to the Federal Parliament the following proposals for putting into effect the principles stated in the Final Act.

The Final Act is concerned with the security of European nations and with their cooperation in all essential spheres. It recognizes that they have a common interest in solving some very important problems. We believe, in particular, that all European nations should work toward controlling the unbridled development of science and technology for the benefit of all mankind.

Czechoslovakia is a highly developed country located in the heart of Europe. Its history shows that its people love progress and freedom and that they can achieve the goals that were set in Helsinki. However, for Czechoslovakia to become a free and open society, radical change is needed.

Present conditions are in glaring contradiction to the principles of the Final Act. The occupation of our country by armies of the Warsaw Pact nations violated the U.N. Charter and, in particular, the principle of national sovereignty, which requires each nation to respect territorial boundaries, individual self-determination, and free elections, and to renounce violence in its dealings with other nations and not interfere in their internal affairs. Moreover, it violates the Warsaw Pact of 1955, which upholds ideals similar to those of the U.N. Charter.

These ideals have often been reaffirmed by the United Nations. In 1959 the Soviet Union proposed a general denunciation of all interference in the internal affairs of nations and promoted the principle of national independence. There have been many other statements advocating friendly relations between countries. Yet the occupation of Czechoslovakia proves that these commitments were empty.

Armies of the Soviet Union still occupy Czechoslovakia and their presence is sanctioned by documents Czechoslovakia was forced to sign after the occupation itself, when hundreds of thousand of foreign troops, armed to the teeth, imposed themselves on us. Representatives of the same five nations whose armies presently occupy our country have now signed an agreement in Helsinki in which they have once again committed themselves to the principle of national sovereignty and to all derivative rights. Furthermore, they have agreed that any threat or application of violence in international affairs, regardless of the circumstance, is unjustifiable. Through its highest representatives the Soviet Union has said time and again that it will comply with these agreements. We believe that it must do so at once if it wants to establish real peace in Europe.

While it is crucial that Czechoslovakia be recognized as a sovereign state, it is no less important that the rights and freedoms of its citizens be honored, as is stated in the Final Act. Also, Czechsolovakia's Constitution (paragraph 20) provides that all citizens should have equal rights and duties and advocates the liberation of the individual from all forms of oppression. It upholds the right to work, to receive an education, and to express one's views freely; it guarantees freedom of the press and freedom of religion, and the inviolability of the individual, his home, and private correspondence.

The signatories of the Final Act have agreed to comply not only with the U.N. Charter but also with the General Declaration on Human Rights that issued from the International Convention on Human Rights. The latter document supports the right to individual self-determination, which all co-signers of the pact on the political rights of citizens are bound to respect. Moreover, it states that no one should be subjected to arbitrary interference in his private life and that everyone has the right to travel abroad without the fear of being forced into exile. In other words it provides that a person's citizenship cannot be arbitrarily revoked, which is common practice in Czechoslovakia today. For citizens are not permitted to exercise their right to free expression, are not allowed to vote freely for representatives of their choice, and have no say in choosing work or working conditions.

The Federal Parliament must be aware of the fact that since 1968 a large percentage of the population has suffered government reprisals. Some persons have been imprisoned because of their political beliefs. Many highly qualified workers have been fired and forced to make a living in positions that do not give them the opportunity to make use of their knowledge, abilities, and experience.

This form of repression has been suffered by internationally famous writers, artists, and other citizens who have contributed greatly to the cultural and scientific development of Czechoslovakia. Thus it impoverishes the whole society, and the damage done today will be felt for a long time to come.

Despite agreements, commitments, and promises, persecution continues. And it is especially cruel that the children and families of victims must suffer. The Federal Parliament should know that in violation of the Czechoslovak Constitution and other agreements concerning educational discrimination, many children have been denied access to high schools, trade schools, technical institutions, and, especially, universities. Young people who were in their infancy in 1968 and could not have been politically active are affected most. Shall we sit idly as the futures of so many youths are endangered and the development of the exceptionally gifted is stifled? What is the purpose of the repression of a whole generation, and who will benefit by it? And who will bear the burden of responsibility? You cannot avoid answering these questions!

The Federal Parliament must understand that we are speaking not of single infringements on human rights but of systematic violations.

In their declaration of August 6, 1975, the Praesidium of the Central Committee of the Communist Party of Czechoslovakia and the Czechoslovak government stressed that they would honor the principles and resolutions of the Conference on Security and Cooperation in Europe. As the highest political organ of the state and its only legislative body, the Federal Parliament has the right to see that this promise is kept. Moreover, Article 29 of the Constitution states: "Citizens and organizations have the right to address proposals and petitions to their representatives, and state organs are obliged to give them a timely response." Accordingly, we address the following demands to the Federal Parliament:

1. We ask that it review the resolutions of the Conference on Security and Cooperation in Europe as soon as possible.

2. We ask that it expedite the evacuation of Soviet troops and secure our national sovereignty in compliance with the Helsinki agreements.

3. We ask that it restore the basic freedoms and human rights that are guaranteed by the Czechoslovak Constitution, the U.N. Charter, the General Declaration on Human Rights, and the Helsinki Agreements, and that it work for the release and rehabilitation of all political prisoners.

4. We ask that it repeal all laws, decrees, and orders that discriminate against children and adults, and that it guarantee that they will never be enacted again.

> DR. FRANTIŠEK KRIEGEL
> DR. GERTRUDA SEKANINOVÁ-ČAKRTOVÁ
> FRANTIŠEK VODSLOŇ
> Prague
> *November 8, 1975*

Karel Kaplan to the Leadership of the Communist Party and of the Government of Czechoslovakia

After ratifying the Final Act of the Helsinki Conference, representatives of the government have vowed repeatedly to put the provisions of this important document into effect. I would like to submit a proposal that would lead to the gradual implementation of the principles agreed upon at the Helsinki Conference.

1. There are many ways to realize the kind of economic cooperation envisioned in the Final Act. The development of economic contacts with the advanced industrial societies of Europe would benefit Czechsolovakia. We could thereby gain access to advanced technology and modernize our industries. Closer economic and scientific ties with other nations would improve Czechoslovakia's standing in the world and would also help us to make more quickly the necessary changes in the structure of our economy to meet the demand for consumer goods in our society. Thus we would be on the road to solving long-term problems.

2. In accordance with the spirit and the letter of the provisions of the Final Act that refer to freedom of political and religious thought, every citizen should be allowed to discuss and defend his views publicly, as long as he does not advocate fascism, genocide, or war.

3. Since 1969 many people have been imprisoned for political and religious reasons. They would have to be released from prison and rehabilitated for the ideals of the Final Act to be

realized. Also, more than ten thousand people have been persecuted because of their political views. They have been fired from their jobs, and their rights have been infringed upon. This persecution has had serious consequences even for their children. The government should restore the rights of these citizens and make sure that they are rehired. It will also be necessary to make changes in the penal law, so that those who express views that differ from the official line will be protected and not considered criminals.

3. In order to facilitate travel abroad for personal or professional reasons, every citizen should be issued a passport. (The Final Act specifies this.) The current practice of giving separate exit permits should be abolished. This is particularly important to travelers who wish to visit their relatives abroad.

4. The Final Act encourages international cooperation. The government should allow free cultural exchange and permit intellectuals and artists to develop contacts with their colleagues in the international community. To make this possible, it should abolish political discrimination in cultural affairs. The ban against certain Czechoslovak authors, filmmakers, and playwrights must be lifted. The Final Act clearly states that every author has the right to have his work published both at home and abroad.

5. For scientific research to make headway, the discrimination against certain scientists must be stopped. All interested parties should have access to all scientific information. Here again, banning orders would have to be lifted. Scientists should have the right to publish the results of their research at home and abroad, regardless of their political convictions.

6. The Final Act puts great emphasis on the free exchange of information between nations. Thus, there should be an end to the current practice of allowing a select group of individuals to decide which articles and stories will be made available to the general public. The censorship of all media must be stopped. Information agencies, the press, radio, and television must be allowed to operate in a way that will give the citizenry unrestricted access to all local, national, and international news. Foreign newspapers and magazines should not be banned. And all Czechoslovak periodicals, including those published during

the Prague Spring, should be made available in both libraries and stores. The government should stop interfering with foreign radio broadcasts. The money saved could be put to better use. We could modernize our communications facilities.

7. The Final Act is a product of the relaxation of tensions in the international political arena, and it opens the door to further progress. The negotiations between the great world powers will undoubtedly lead to the curtailment of expenditures for arms. This should help solve some of our economic problems, for more revenue will be available for peacetime use.

8. Czechoslovakia would contribute much to the easing of political tensions in Europe and to cooperation between nations if it repealed all laws introduced since the military occupation of 1968.

I regard this proposal as only the first step in initiating a dialogue with the political leadership. Its consideration would serve as proof that the government seriously intends to respect the principles of the Final Act. When it does, it will contribute to the cooperation of all European governments. I am prepared to submit more proposals and drafts of new legislation at any time.

KAREL KAPLAN

4

Letters and Declarations to Foreigners

It is no accident that the documents contained in this chapter were written in the past three years. The opposition has always recognized both the importance of making the West aware of Czechoslovak problems and the political considerations involved in this. The fact that right-wing periodicals like *Bild Zeitung* in West Germany defended Dubček, after the occupation of Czechoslovakia by the Warsaw Pact countries, had a negative effect on the opposition. Also, from the very beginning the reform Communists who were expelled from the Party posed questions about their alliances.

When international tensions were first relaxed, Western political parties and governments were cautious about commenting on the internal problems of socialist countries so as not to threaten any progress that was being made. And the socialist countries on their part, arguing that criticism from abroad constituted "interference in their internal affairs," almost always ignored suggestions from the outside on principle. However, the agreement ratified by thirty-five governments in Helsinki in 1975 substantially weakened this argument.

A declaration like the Helsinki Agreement is meaningful only if its implementation is supervised and controlled. Thus, during the Conference the Soviet Union insisted that an international organization be established to determine whether or not the commitments made in Helsinki were being fulfilled. The final result of this attempt was the decision to hold another conference after two years to discuss progress in international relations.

It was then that the Czechoslovak opposition began to write to foreign politicians, colleagues, and political organizations in order to familiarize them with the conditions in Czechoslovakia. In many cases they wrote to professional colleagues. Dramatist Pavel Kohout wrote immediately after the Helsinki Conference to his foreign colleagues Arthur Miller and Heinrich Böll (as representatives of the authors of the countries present at the Conference), proposing that a European Cultural Conference be organized, at which specific cultural problems between the East and the West could be discussed. Initially, such a proposition may seem Utopian, yet it is based on the very practical consideration that the political implications of the Act could be applied to specific areas. The Czechoslovak opposition was the first in Eastern Europe to conclude that certain political questions, which before the Helsinki meeting had been dealt with only within a factional framework, could now be put into an international context. The Communists in the Czechoslovak opposition intensified their contact with other Communist parties in Europe, and this became the basis for an alliance between the Czechoslovak opposition and the Communist parties of Italy, Spain, and France. As a result, when the Communist Party of Czechoslovakia began a campaign of oppression immediately after the publication of Charter '77, the Eurocommunist parties criticized it sharply.

Again and again the mobilization of Western public opinion—primarily through prominent figures—has had an impact in Prague. There is no doubt that the sentences in the trial of the young pop musicians in Prague were lighter than what the prosecutors were demanding because of the widespread reaction from the West. A letter from a group of Czechoslovak intellectuals to Heinrich Böll, and his reply to the poet Jaroslav Seifert, contributed greatly to this publicity.

Vilém Prečan, a historian, who was forbidden to teach or do research, wrote to the World Congress of Historians in San Francisco, drawing attention to the position of his colleagues in Czechoslovakia. This letter was widely covered in the world press, and the show of solidarity between historians eventually led to permission for Prečan and his family to leave the country. Individual expressions of solidarity have also been helpful, as in the case of the philosopher Karel Kosík, who had a one thousand-page manuscript that had been confiscated returned to him by the police after he wrote his open letter to Jean-Paul Sartre.

HANS-PETER RIESE

Karel Kosík
to Jean-Paul Sartre

Dear Jean-Paul Sartre,

The event that I am writing about in this letter is completely banal and would not appeal to the tabloids. Thus I do not address myself to an anonymous sensationalist, but to you and, with your help, to my socialist, democratic, and Communist friends who are also friends of Czechoslovakia. I am writing neither an appeal nor a protest; only a simple, but for me, vital question:

Am I guilty?

This question has plagued me ever since April 28, 1975, when the police took six hours to search my home and finally confiscated more than one thousand pages of my philosophical manuscript. This search was based on the suspicion that I was "hiding" papers in my apartment, which constitutes the punishable act of trying "to overthrow the republic." I must assume that I shall be sentenced to a maximum of five years in prison —this is what the appropriate paragraph (No. 98) of the penal code demands; and while I do not underestimate this threat, it is the fate of the confiscated manuscript that is nearest my heart.

During the past six years I have existed in a special situation and in two-fold form: I am, yet at the same time I am not. I am dead and alive simultaneously: on one hand, I have been reduced to nothing as far as basic civil and human rights are concerned, and yet at the same time I am considered to be of extraordinary importance as far as the care and attention of the police go. I am a mere nothing, and therefore cannot teach philosophy at Charles University, nor can I be employed anywhere else in a position appropriate to my abilities and my field. I am dead and must therefore not participate in any of the scientific conventions to which I am invited; nor can I accept any invitations to lecture at European universities.

As one who does not exist, and basically has never existed, I am not permitted to mislead our country's readers, and so all my publications have been banned in Czechoslovakia. My name has been eliminated from the nation's list of authors. I do not exist, and therefore the official institutions are not obliged to answer my complaints and my protests. Yet, in another respect I exist too much, as the search of my home and now regular interrogations by the police are proving. As an author and a philosopher I have been buried alive; as a citizen I have been deprived of my basic rights, and I am living as one who is permanently accused and suspected.

I am suspected, although I did not commit a punishable act. Why, then, am I under suspicion? It is because I regard thinking as an inalienable human right and make use of this right? Because I think that everyone has the right to have his own opinion and to express this opinion and communicate it? Because I also consider the right to self-respect to be inalienable?

Why am I a suspicious character? Because under certain conditions, in an atmosphere of general suspicion, the basic elements of human conduct and values that are inherent in the overwhelming majority of mankind—values like friendship, honor, humor, a sense of decency, and truth—are seen as eccentric and provocative, and normal words and feelings take on their opposite meanings. The simple sentence, "I have sprained my ankle and must limp," becomes a subversive remark in the ears of the police, and one who appears to limp is regarded by them as pretending in order to conceal some "dark acts." In such an atmosphere even established rights are immediately curtailed or completely eliminated. Everyone has the right to think, but one who thinks without permission and without order, or who does not think as one is supposed to think, stirs up suspicion. Everyone may have his own views, but one who refuses to take on the alien and unproven views that are forced upon him as his own, one who insists on rational, open argument, will be suspect. Everyone has the right to self-respect, but one who does not "voluntarily" subliminate his self-respect to humiliating repentance and fawning thankfulness has no hope of publishing his work or being employed according to his abilities.

The confiscated manuscript was not meant to be published. It contained unedited notes, studies in preparation, and outlines for two books I wanted to publish, *On Practice* and *On Truth*. The manuscript contained only private opinions, either of others of no interest to the police, or of my own, which the police already know from my earlier books and essays. I would like to believe the police officer who assured me that the manuscript would be returned after careful scrutiny, but how long will they "study" one thousand pages of my philosophical writings? And there are still other, more serious circumstances in that the police also confiscated the manuscripts of my friends Ivan Klíma and Ludvík Vaculík, both writers. I am beginning to wonder if I was a witness last April to an event that may have the most serious repercussions.

Were not the effects and implications of the methods used on that day so great that, comparatively speaking, the prevailing practice of censorship is no more than child's play? Was this act in April 1975 not an attempt to impose a new custom and a new norm upon the society: the periodic confiscation of manuscripts? Is it not possible that in a short time we will be living in a Kafkaesque world where, as a matter of course, the authors themselves will call the police out of an indoctrinated need to have their work taken from them?

I am not a supporter of such a novelty.

As I have already mentioned, up until now I have not received a response to my request for the return of my work. I have remained silent in the face of all of these discriminatory practices, never protesting publicly, because the discrimination was directed only against myself and did not threaten the essence of my existence— the opportunity to think and to write. This time, however, I cannot remain silent, because *I don't want to be guilty.* And I would become an accessory to the crime if I remained silent and watched and waited as the Sword of Damocles hung over the heads of all Czech writers and the police chose the person, time, and place for the confiscation of manuscripts, finished or otherwise.

We still have time to avoid this threat. I have not lost hope in the prudence of responsible officials, and I continue to trust in the farsightedness and conscience of the socialist, Communist, and democratic friends of Czechoslovakia.

Please accept, dear friend, my heartiest greetings.

KAREL KOSÍK
Prague
May 26, 1975

Jean-Paul Sartre to Karel Kosík

Dear Friend,

The reason I have not written to you in such a long time is very simple: Your open letter was not delivered to me. I read only a short excerpt from it in *Le Monde,* and the original was very difficult to get hold of. But finally I got it and can now answer your question directly: No, you are not guilty. Your letter is sufficient proof of this, not only for me but for all friends of the humiliated, occupied country of Czechoslovakia.

If I am sure of anything in this life, it is that the most basic right of any human being is the ability to think for himself. To the extent that I—or anyone—have defended views held by a group of men, I have always done so because these views penetrated me: because I compared them with my own views, evaluated them, and accepted them. In short, they became my views. No government is entitled to condemn the ideas of its citizens. After all, the government would not condemn such ideas from the point of view of thinking, but from that of pseudo-thinking.

For me, real ideas are only concepts that have their roots in human beings themselves, or concepts from outside sources that we have judged freely and, when found to be correct, then accepted as such. The views that your government holds I would call pseudoviews: They are not the product of free-thinking people, nor are they examined by free people. They consist of groups of words, chosen in the Soviet Union, words that conceal that country's deeds so as not to reveal their true nature. Such ideas are not a force that can prevail without the help of another real, material, and well-known force: the police. To this force, the criminal political leaders have tried to subject the Czechoslovak culture.

Something so shameless and stupid cannot last long, as long as people like you, my friend, exist to expose them for what they are. The police may continue to suppress free thinking for a time, but this is also a means for people to realize the situation they are living in. Thus, in the last analysis the only hope of the ruling powers is either to eliminate these people or to do away with their false ideas.

Of course, I can guarantee only my own support. But for some time I have been having discussions with people about your dear and unhappy country, and I can assure you that you have many friends who would shout together with me: "If Karel Kosík is guilty, then everyone (not only the intellectuals but also the farmers and workers) who thinks about what he is doing, is guilty as well."

This simple thought must become the point of departure for actions we shall decide to take in order to, while helping you, also help ourselves.

With my feelings of sincere brotherhood,

Yours,
JEAN-PAUL SARTRE
Paris
June 26, 1975

Pavel Kohout to Heinrich Böll and Arthur Miller

Dear Heinrich Böll and Arthur Miller,

I am addressing myself to you—as my friends who know who I am and how I think, and also as important authors who have contributed to the fact that our world is not worse than it is—in order to, with your help, address all my colleagues in the so-called "East" and "West."

I do not intend to write a political manifesto or, for that matter, a complaint; everything I am going to say has been spoken of either by me or by my fellow citizens. I do not intend to pour more oil on the fires of controversy. My concern is with a way out of a situation that is common not only to Czechoslovakia, a situation produced by a social movement and a power conflict; it has happened in the past, it exists now, and it will happen again.

For seven years dozens of Czech and Slovak writers have lived and worked under conditions that are the result of events that occurred in 1968. Whether these events and our participation in them are to be evaluated as positive or negative, one thing is generally known: we have never violated the law or the ethics of writers with our activities. We engaged ourselves in ideas that have been temporarily suppressed by the powers that be; that is all.

Direct reprisal has taken the form of electronic and human surveillance, interrogations, home search, and arrest.

We do not regard this treatment as a special favor on the government's part; it is simply an expression of the fact that the state is aware of how difficult it would be to prove to the nation and the world that we violated the law. Although we have been accused of committing the most absurd sins, we really could do no more than to stay at home and continue to work.

One would expect that such behavior and attitude—our attempt to participate in the development of our national culture even under conditions of disgrace—would be understood by the regime as an expression of good will: the more so since the regime has always claimed that it enjoys the united support of the entire population. Our opposition focuses on the methods, rather than the goals, of the leadership.

However, after seven years we and the regime have arrived back at the beginning of the circle: We bear the fate of those who are forced to be silent, and as part of the silencing the regime reaps the shame of its decision to offer some of us passports out of the country as the only solution. Aside from the threat of losing one's citizenship, being forced to leave the country means to be torn out of one's domestic context and is actually silencing in another form.

In this clash of wills there are no victors or vanquished, only the fallen, those who were not able to resist physically and those who could not resist spiritually. The humiliating self-criticism that follows, even when it is dictated by human motives—the desire to publish, or to allow one's children to go to school—is the saddest of all: A grown man, who in a single press release renounces everything he has stood for all his life, loses in that moment the esteem of his friends, his readers, and, most of all, of the regime, which knows full well what has caused this "insight" and what little weight it has. And, finally, there is the loss of self-esteem, unless the individual, reacting defensively, becomes cynical. But I wonder which is worse?

Some writers, myself included, have been lucky enough to have their works published abroad. Lucky, I should say, insofar as it is encouraging to know that we have some communication with the world and that despite restrictions, we continue to exist as writers. However, from the point of view of what is essential in literature, which is, after all, the product of the spirit and language of a specific community and must be evaluated first of all by that community, we are on the same level as those who are writing for the bureau drawer. And if there are too many drawers, or if the drawer-epoch should last too long without the hope of change, then serious structural disturbances of not only literature but the whole culture will result. This is the more dangerous because it may coincide with the further development of technology and an increasing consumerism. Václav Havel discussed this possibility in depth in his open letter to Dr. Gustáv Husák in April; I warmly recommend that letter to your attention.

Both of you, dear Heinrich Böll and Arthur Miller, know our situation very well. You witnessed its start and development and know that we remained faithful to our convictions, although we restricted ourselves to defending only the most monstrous injustices. It was because of this that, for instance, on the recommendations of my friends I apologized to Günter Grass for not answering his open letter about democratic socialism that appeared in *Die Zeit.*

I have subordinated everything to one goal: writing. I knew that by doing so it might be possible for me to have at least an elementary communication with my closest circle of readers. In the age of rotary presses and the most modern forms of printing, dozens of mature, well-known writers have been forced to write as they did in their student years: We have had to transcribe copies of manuscripts and give them or "sell" them at cost to our friends. This is not illegal, because each copy is signed by its author, and neither is it a game: Today, these "free editions" amount to more than fifty titles by nearly thirty authors. Furthermore, to give ourselves the opportunity to reflect on simple human things— the opportunity newspapers once offered us—we have begun to write essays and stories, newspaper features really, about spring, Easter, or the beginning of human culture, and we send them regularly to each other. These texts, signed by the authors of course, are circulating with such speed that they defy the official statement that their authors are not accepted by the nation.

The age of innocence for these manuscripts, however, ended in April of this year, when teams of State Security agents searched the homes of my colleagues and other citizens for the express purpose of confiscating these manuscripts. This action culminated in the confiscation, under orders, of works that had only been begun, including the one thousand pages of philosophical notes from the home of Karel Kosík.

This event moved me deeply. I expected that my colleagues would at least get an answer to their requests for their manuscripts' return, but this has not happened, and now I feel threatened in the same way as my friends. Is this not a precedent for future action, so that the police may come and simply take whatever they like? Shall I begin to put my signature on each page of my writing and hide all the pages each evening?

The devil's circle is completed. According to the authorities, only those who write are writers, and, in order to prevent people who are disliked by the regime from writing, a total ban on publications by these authors has been imposed. Now even manuscripts are being confiscated in order to make writing completely impossible. This is why I am writing this letter, and I would like to pose the following questions to you and my international colleagues:

1. Is it possible that any writer deserving of the name would not think and write about the conflicts in his society, even if his opinions, at a particular moment, differ from those of the people in power? Does he thereby commit an offense against the state?

2. Does any government signing the Charter of Human Rights have the right to silence an artist simply because he is "guilty of independent thinking"? Is it permissible to deprive him of his right to publish his work even in the most primitive form of a transcript?

3. Does the government have the right to confiscate a manuscript on which an author is working, one that has not been

published even in transcript form? What is the difference between such a manuscript and a mere thought?

4. Is it possible that in a world where even criminals are allowed to return to a normal life after their release from prison, a ban of unlimited duration can be imposed on the work of a specific author or on a great part of a nation's literature?

5. Is this a form of apartheid or not?

6. Is it possible that international literary and cultural organizations, including UNESCO, will take no notice of this situation?

7. Is it possible to have any European cooperation at all in the area of culture without attempting to eliminate such practices and guaranteeing that they will never be repeated?

We are living in a time when not only artists and scientists but statesmen as well are inclined to the view that controversial questions should be solved by negotiation rather than by force. The organization of the Conference for Security and Cooperation in Europe is the best proof of this. We have seen the way in which statesmen involve themselves in problems that do not touch their own nations directly because they believe that peace is indivisible and belongs to all of us. In my mind, culture is also indivisible and belongs to all of us.

I grew up with Hašek and Čapek, Stendhal and Majakowski, and, as a dramatist, with Dürrenmatt and Shaw. The Czech Jan Neruda lent his name to the great Chilean poet, and Franz Kafka influenced the world of literature as only a few have. Is there a reason why writers, even though they are not touched (for the moment) by the problems of their colleagues abroad, should not be engaged in the solution of these problems?

The situation now facing Czech and Slovak literature cries out for such a mission. Couldn't you, dear Heinrich Böll and Arthur Miller, and with you our other colleagues from the countries participating in the Conference, come to Prague and Bratislava, listen to the different views, and attempt to help us negotiate a *modus vivendi* for this and similar situations in the future? A government that honestly undertakes the peaceful solution of bloody conflicts between nations or different social orders could not prosecute the adherents of opposing principles when they are engaged in the issue of a bloodless conflict of different views between groups of citizens! And if such an attempted visit fails, would it not be possible, at the initiative of writers and their organizations, to hold a European or even a world conference concerned with the role and mission of culture in an era of consumer technology, or with the effective solution of the conflict between power and culture, issues that will confront all of us in different parts of the world for many years to come? At the very least, we in Czechoslovakia could participate in the discussions, if only from a distance.

Our predecessors, the Czech and Slovak writers between the two World Wars, Communists like Kisch and democrats like Čapek, did everything possible to help the endangered German culture. And with our proclamations as well as with concrete actions over many years, my generation supported all of our colleagues who tried to maintain the continuity of their national culture in hard times. Some of them remained at home, like the victims of McCarthyism in the United States, while others found refuge in our country: I met Pablo Neruda in Prague, and Nazim Hikmet was my friend. Don't we, as socialists in a socialist country, deserve friendly advice and help in our time of trouble? Admittedly, we are not fighting for our lives, but we are fighting for our right to be writers.

Finally, I should explain, dear Heinrich Böll and Arthur Miller, why I am addressing this open letter, meant for so many people, directly to both of you: it is because the accredited agencies of the foreign press in Prague have joined our authorities in their attempts to hamper our communication with the outside world. In order to avoid trouble they have agreed—God knows on whose initiative—on a common procedure on the forwarding of our letters: either all or none. The second alternative is generally preferred, and even if they doubt the sense of their mission, they have introduced a second censorship barrier, one even more absurd than the first.

Therefore I have had to look for a new means of communication, and I ask you, my two friends, whom I respect as much as authors as I do as human beings, to make my letter and my questions public, in whatever form you choose, so that my colleagues and writers' associations and other European cultural communities will become acquainted with their content.

I am doing this not for myself but for all of us. And I am doing it convinced that it is a serious affair, of concern to you, as well as to all others.

With regards and in expectation of your reply,

Yours,
PAVEL KOHOUT
Prague,
June 9, 1975

Ludvík Vaculík to Kurt Waldheim, Secretary General of the United Nations

Dear Mr. Secretary General,

In our neighboring countries, which were for some time united, it used to be a custom to introduce a letter with many wishes: God's mercy, the assistance of the patron Saints, patience in times of ordeal, and good health. In our materialist time, Mr. Secretary General, I wish you at the very least, patience in ordeals, good health, and heavenly assistance.

I am writing to you after much consideration as to whether or not it is proper to do so. A quarter of a year has passed since an event that touched me very deeply. I considered writing you at that time but rejected the thought as eccentric; a sober inner voice told me, "Don't be insane! What actually happened to you? They broke into your apartment, rummaged through your life, and took away some of your belongings. Be patient." I was offended by this action but at the same time glad that nothing worse had happened. However, as the months have passed, I have become aware of how I am living these days: with the constant fear that they may come again, or ask me to call on them, and with a feeling of miserable gratefulness for each day when nothing happens.

I came to the decision to write you for the following reasons: My anger and resentment have remained and are growing; the time I gave the authorities in my own mind to tell me what crime I had committed or to send me apologies, has passed, and in the meantime something else has happened that

I take as a further warning—the joint flight of the spaceships *Apollo* and *Soyuz*.

In April of this year you were in Prague. Charles University endowed you with an honorary Doctorate of Law, complementing your Viennese doctorate, and on this occasion you said, "Some two-thirds of the world are living under conditions unknown in any developed country." Both of our countries belong to the developed world and, viewed from this angle, are regarded as the spoiled ones. This sometimes evokes a feeling of guilt in many of us, ranging from guilt for crimes actually committed to those metaphysical in nature. And persons who are guilty should be silent out of decency and not dare to join in an indictment of others.

Because of this I often say to myself ironically that I, or we, have what we wanted (as was written in a Czech people's song in the late forties), and therefore we should not hold someone else responsible for the conditions under which we have to live. As a Czech I share the responsibility for the disintegration of the Austrian-Hungarian monarchy, which took place long before I was born. In my younger days I also fought in the Second World War and then participated in the creation of two separate zones in Europe. Now I have the shared responsibility for the Conference in Helsinki hanging over my head, and who knows what consequences will come of that. Finally, as a former member of the Communist Party of Czechoslovakia I am an accessory to the reality produced by the collective ideals of social justice and an allegedly higher form of democracy, the "peoples'" democracy.

I cannot trace a direct political guilt: I never enjoyed the faith of the Party enough for them to offer me even the smallest official function; as a journalist and a writer I belonged to His Majesty's inner opposition. (Yet this is balanced by my moral guilt.) I don't feel I am a criminal, but this is exactly the charge the government wants to force on me. And I am angry at this and call people names; but somewhere deeper, in that metaphysical side of me, I am not that angry: I assume that this is how it is in the world today, and that perhaps this is how it should be. The problem is that we all, you and I and all of us, behave more like our real selves than our ideal selves in the harsh reality of day-to-day living. That is what makes it so difficult to live peaceably with someone who is our enemy; this is something that I am sure you, Mr. Secretary General, are well acquainted with.

It is a difficult case for a lawyer. In the fall of 1969 I was indicted for undermining the republic because I co-authored a petition addressed to the highest state authorities. In this petition I expressed my dissatisfaction with the development of conditions in our country since August of 1968. By the fall of 1970 the eight co-authors of this petition had been indicted and a trial was supposed to take place, but the day before the date set, the trial was postponed and the public was told that no trial was foreseen; it was all supposedly the invention of slanderers.

In the fall of 1973 criminal procedures were again initiated against me, this time for my participation in an interview with the BBC. Yet these proceedings must be trapped somewhere in limbo, for I have never been indicted for my alleged offense. As of this writing, the investigation has been neither stopped nor repealed; no one has told me anything, and I don't know where the indictment stands, or even where it would stand if I was living under some normal system of laws. I know that they have taken my passport, demoted me from lieutenant to ordinary soldier (which I didn't mind), and put me under the kind of surveillance that involves tampering with all of my communications (mail, telephone, contacts with foreigners, social and sexual relations, and so on) in order to undermine my social contacts and other activities and, in effect, reduce my life to those few survival functions that are of no real importance.

Quite frankly, I would like to know what is going on. (I should add that once a criminal proceeding has been initiated, an arrest may follow at any time, based on, say, a "continuation of punishable activities," such as another interview with a foreign broadcasting company, or even a letter to the United Nations.) What do we call this kind of situation? Is there a concept, some example in legal terminology, that would describe these activities in peacetime?

I suspect that the so-called "trial" actually did take place in 1970, and that it took place without public witnesses and without defendants. Not in a courthouse, however, but in some unknown building, in a dusty attic, as prophetically described by Franz Kafka. There, both I and my sons were sentenced to an unknown punishment for an unknown period of time.

Mr. Secretary General, I have just noticed that in my attempt to describe to you what has been happening to me, I automatically, logically, and truthfully let slip some words about my sons. I have three, and the thought of them lessens my anger and frustration somewhat at this moment. It brings me back to a higher understanding of things and to the thought that everything that happens has a reason for happening, and perhaps has been caused by us and is purposeful and significant. I don't think that it is a misfortune when children share the fate of their parents—it would be worse if the children were permitted to live their lives separately; in that way the continuum of the consciousness of a species, of a nation, and of the population of a continent would be interrupted. I think (Shame!—but I am gloating!) that even if the state excludes a child from its mercy, it does so against its better judgment, believing that this is a better method of ensuring that a germ of future dignity and courage for the nation remains in its subjects than risking its fate to the natural development of human nature. Or do you think that I am just trying to console myself, allowing that well-known need of ironical troublemakers and skeptical optimists to break through? If this is true, I guess I didn't understand the statement you made in Prague as you were waiting for your honorary doctorate: "The situation in the world that disturbs us, at the same time also gives us hope."

Toward the end of April of this year a group of employees of the State Security Agency came to search my apartment. They did so with the approval of the General Prosecutor, as it was suspected that I might have hidden some secret written material, thus proving that the punishable act of undermining the Republic had occurred. Who actually committed this punishable act, I was not told. According to the new Penal Code, even if I myself am not the alleged culprit, it is still possible to look in my apartment for proof of the act. Thus, it is permissible to search my apartment whether something is to be found there or not. Is this possible in any country in peacetime? Or at least in any country in Europe?

During the search many of my possessions were taken away: most of my books, some newspapers, notes, manuscripts borrowed from and belonging to my friends, letters, photographs, and tapes; they did not find anything that could be classified as "illegal printed matter." Since that time, though no one has spoken directly to me, at least fifteen people that I know of have been interrogated about me. Further, none of the confiscated material has been returned, and my complaint to the General Prosecutor about the laws violated by this action was turned over to the very people I was complaining about.

Among the papers I have lost is a manuscript I have been working on for some years. It is a novel describing actions of long-lasting impact, filled with observations and meditations; it is about landscapes, people, and history. I am afraid it will not become a best seller, but I think it should become a Czech book; I am hoping that it will interest a few reflective people in the plain between the Alps, the Carpathians, and the Sudetes. I don't know how the book is going to end, or what I was going to add or to delete, but according to Czechoslovak security it is already a shocking book. Because of this, if I were to lend the book to my friends or publish it abroad, I would be committing the crime of instigating a rebellion.

I should explain that in Czechoslovakia such a crime is committed when the "instigation," in whatever form, has been communicated to at least two persons. Therefore, it would be sufficient if I gave the manuscript to my secretary to transcribe and then to my friend Karel Kosík (whose philosophical notes have also been confiscated). I don't know how things are in Vienna, but in the Charles University in Prague they are learning that "the preparation for a punishable act is to be punished with the punishment prescribed for the punishable act" (Chapter 2, paragraph 7 of the Penal Code). Thus, when I write a "shocking" book with the intention (naturally) that someone shall read it, I am making preparations for a punishable act. This is not a literary overstatement but a matter of fact and of logical deduction. The following, with your permission, is a literary overstatement:

If, by an evil twist of fate, you had not been endowed with an honorary doctorate but had instead graduated from Charles

University like anyone else, you would have become a judge. In this capacity you would be obliged, despite the six-hundred-year-old tradition of the University, to sentence quite a number of Czech authors to three years in prison (see paragraph 100 of the Penal Code) for the discovery of manuscripts on their desks, and from three to five years if they had tried to present their manuscripts for publication. If one of these authors happened to be me, with two unfinished penal proceedings to his name, you would sentence me to the "palette," excuse me, the full amount of punishment.

You must forgive me, Mr. Secretary General, for putting such an abominable notion in your mind, but at least now you know what kind of man I am, and how I excite people. I only wanted to make clear the difference between the two types of doctorates that are now available in our dear old plains between the Alps, the Carpathians, and the Sudetes. I am truly sorry, and, as an expression of my belief that you would never become this kind of judge, I must tell you a secret: There really were things in my confiscated manuscript that are mutinous as far as our conditions are concerned. But you must understand me— I wrote them because I was under the impression that I was at home in the privacy of my apartment, that no one would see me, and no one hear me. I might have written out of anger, or melancholy, but I don't remember. I just felt free to put down on paper what I wanted to, as if it had been before the war. Or at the time of the Austrian-Hungarian monarchy. Or as if it were peacetime.

Since the wartime event of April of this year, I cannot think peacefully about the confiscated book that I had only begun to write. Every time I put paper in my typewriter, nothing but a protest will come out. While the whole world is excited and encouraged by the Americans and the Russians working together in space, I continue with my petty concern for my papers and my other belongings, trying to develop legal tactics to bring about their return, even though I am only a layman when it comes to law. And this is the meaning of my letter to you, Mr. Secretary General: I ask you to think about what I have written, and, if you find that my letter is deserving, please give it to a team of expert lawyers and ask them for their opinions.

All governments, insofar as they want to appear in good company and attend those solemn international conferences, find it proper to guarantee personal freedom in their constitutions. This freedom is part of the word "Europe," and the greatest invention in our history. In my opinion, the times require that this invention be somehow better cared for. I must ask where the personality of a human being ends: at his nose, at his heels, or at the first stroke of his pen? Until recently, it seemed to me permissible for human beings to shift their thoughts from one side of their heads to the other. But are they also allowed to put them on paper on their desks, to run their eyes over them, and to arrange them?

In my country, Dr. Waldheim, these questions are debatable, and I am reporting this to you because it may become an ugly European precedent if it is not stopped. It will not be as simple as the return of my papers, or Kosík's, or the others' (and there are many others). More has to happen. If it doesn't, I see no guarantee that the next time the police come to my apartment in order to preserve law and order in the country, they will not say, "What are you thinking? Come with us!"

And this will be the first step toward the practice in all countries of putting small machines into the heads of newborn babies to prevent thoughts from being shifted from the right hemisphere of the brain to the left. Later, these machines will enable the movements of whole populations to be controlled by two spaceships, one revolving around the Western hemisphere, and the other around the Eastern. These operations will eventually attract no more attention than a vaccination does today. And, of course, this will all take place in the interest of peace and friendship between the nations of the world and to eliminate the danger that somewhere on this planet even a germ of courage or human dignity for the future might be preserved.

My dear Secretary General, this is nearly all of what I think. The rest deals with the metaphysical rather than the practical, and I could tell you about it only if we could both be guaranteed, somewhere on this great plain, at least one square yard of private ground.

I am awaiting your reply. In the meantime, I wish you

continued belief in the meaning—and the success—of your work. And most important—lest I forget—I wish you good health, patience in times of ordeal, and the heavenly assistance of the patron Saints.

With due respect,
LUDVÍK VACULÍK
Prague
July 29, 1975

Vilém Prečan to the Participants of the World Congress of Historians in San Francisco, August 1975

My Dear Colleagues,

As many of you may remember, five years ago at the World Congress of Historians in Moscow, an "incident" occurred: Professor Eberhard Jäckel from the University in Stuttgart protested against the prosecution and dismissal of some Czechoslovak historians. None of the representatives of those militant forces that were instrumental in the "purifying" of Czech universities and scientific institutions through the dismissal of dozens of historians in 1970 dared to answer in the name of the Czechoslovak historians present at the conference. Instead, they sent someone who enjoys authority among his foreign colleagues to express his regret at Professor Jäckel's political remarks.

I had the opportunity to ask Jiří Kořalka, the Czech historian who attacked Professor Jäckel, whether he acted legitimately at that time or only to save himself, as he also was threatened by the "purification." In any case, the past five years has proved that Professor Jäckel, and not Jiří Kořalka, was right.

I would like to express my gratitude to all who have protested against the persecution of Czechoslovak intellectuals in the past few years, against what is already the third persecution since 1938. Out of my own personal experience, I can confirm what the support of my colleagues abroad has meant to me, both personally and professionally. The manifestation of their solidarity, friendship, and help in different forms has enabled me to survive the hardest years since the loss of my employment. This made it possible for me to bear the persecution of a totalitarian regime, to maintain close contact with free and critical thinking in the world, and to continue to be a historian, at least in my free time.

The world was not silent four years ago when the Czechoslovak Prosecutor General and the Czechoslovak Security Service (the secret police) began their criminal proceedings against me and my closest friends. We were accused of participating in the editing and publication of the document, "Seven Days in Prague: August 21–27, 1968," which was, rightly or wrongly, declared to be a "Black Book." Except for these outside protests, everything pointed to my inevitable imprisonment.

I want to thank my colleagues A. P. J. Taylor and R. L. Trevor-Roper, who were the first to register a protest in the *Times* of London against the persecution of the authors and publishers of the Black Book. I would also like to thank all who followed them, especially F. W. Carsten at the University of London and my colleagues at St. Antony's College, Oxford, who received me as their guest in 1969 and have made me feel that they regard me as their "fellow" ever since.

During my interrogation by the State Security Agency I was shown, among other things, the American Historical Association's letter addressed to the representatives of the Czechoslovak Academy of Science. I thank the executive committee of the Association from the bottom of my heart. Its speaker, Paul L. Ward, wrote that "in the name of science and humanity" it was expected that "due respect" would be shown toward "scientific publication of documents for the information of future generations," and that consequently the authors of this publication should not be tried. I cannot forget the absurd remarks of my interrogators in describing this letter as proof "that the publication, 'Seven Days in Prague' served, and still serves, the bourgeois ideologists as a provocation for emotion and anti-socialist sentiments."

I am sure that there were more declarations of solidarity and protests against the persecution of historians. I was not aware of all of them, so I am unable to thank each individual. When I openly express my gratitude at this time, I do so for serious reasons. My friends, whom I have met in the past six years in Prague, know very well that I never humiliated myself under pressure. I did everything to maintain my personal and scientific integrity, and I never gave up what I regard to be the right and duty of an historian.

Still, I never published an official declaration, not only because I do not like the limelight of official tribunes and because, as an ordinary historian, I never felt the need to make use of one, but also because I wanted to avoid any direct conflict with the authorities. Even when everything seems to have been taken, one still has something to lose; even when these brutal forces take away the possibility of employment, forcing one—after twenty years of study and creative work—to perform slave labor, even when those few rights the general population still possesses are removed, even when one is interrogated like a criminal for his actions as an historian.

I did not emigrate during the years when it was possible to do so, even though I had every opportunity. Even in 1969 I thought I would be able to continue the work I had started at home and to defend my right to do creative work. I also wanted to protect my own work, and that of my colleagues, against slander. Even after Czechoslovakia issued a warrant for the arrest of the entire culture (and it became clear that in the conflict between culture and totalitarian power, culture had no chance), there was still something to be done.

A historian knows the past not only from texts and literature. When he is forbidden to study the archives, the world around him becomes his object of study. Thus, Czechoslovakia became my subject: how a society behaves in crisis situations, how institutions and the power apparatus function when a certain type of totalitarian regime is reinstated, how different social groups and individuals behave in difficult circumstances, in true tests of being, in times when all other questions are pushed into the background by a single one; how to survive—as a human being, an intellectual, and thus as a historian, as well.

Yet another factor influenced me. It may seem ridiculous, but for years I worried about what a historian calls his private archives—his notes, excerpts, manuscripts, and documentations collected over many, many years. Without them, I would have felt lost and impoverished. And, as everyone knows, all it takes is a single police action. Afraid of malicious interference or revenge, I addressed my complaints in the form of private letters only and directed those private complaints and petitions to the people in power and to the courts. Even this year, when I was forbidden to earn a living and support my family as a doorman in a pub in Prague, my only protest took the form of a private cable addressed to the political representatives of Czechoslovakia.

And in March of this year I didn't act in a radical way, although I felt I could no longer live without access to archives, books, and newspapers, or without real contact with my colleagues. Fear told me that the Czechoslovak form of apartheid is a life sentence to existential and spiritual atrophy. I wrote a short and courteous letter—only eighteen lines—to the Minister of the Interior, to Dr. G. Husák and to V. Bilak. I asked them whether I might emigrate with my family and could now begin to negotiate with foreign institutions to this end without risking persecution.

The only answer to this inquiry, as to my protests in preceding years, was silence—and a new form of persecution. On April 24, 1975, the police searched my home and gave me the most painful blow of my life: They competed with each other in their eagerness to find what they, in their most absurd language, called "antistate material." They confiscated a part of my library and my archives, my personal diary containing my most private notes, and, a day later, during a search of a friend's home they also took the letters I had written him over the past few years. It was then that I decided to accept the challenge.

I wanted to remain a historian, convinced—and I am not alone in my conviction—that the historian has a duty and responsibility to work. This has been systematically made impossible for me. I longed for nothing more than the peace and privacy of my study and my archives; instead, I am forced to defend myself publicly and scream for help. I wanted to remain in the country I was born in and to work for its good; instead, because they don't allow me to live a normal life here, I am forced to ask for my human right to emigrate.

Dear friends, it has become truly unbearable. Like many of

my colleagues—and so, your colleagues too—I am suffering from the absolute lack of any legal, existential, or personal security. A group of policemen may intrude upon my home at any time with a warrant from the Prosecutor General to search my house or to arrest me. They could come this very moment and confiscate this unfinished letter out of my typewriter. And even if they wait, I know too well the rules of the anachronistic Penal Code, which the police, the prosecutor, and the courts may use against me for having written and mailed this letter; and I know the punishment I could expect. (In this regard, I would like to assure you that the section of the Czechoslovak Penal Code dealing with the so-called "punishable acts against the republic" ridicules the Charter of Human Rights signed by Czechoslovakia. What they call "socialist lawfulness" is, in this context, nothing but a brutal violation of basic human and citizen's rights.)

The political regime that exists in Czechoslovakia is unable to find any way to preserve its existence except police power. Six years have passed since the beginning of the so-called "consolidation," and our situation is now far worse than it was then. It is a crime to own papers other than those permitted by the government, which continues to confiscate books, manuscripts, and personal notices. Czechoslovak intellectuals and others are treated worse than criminals in other countries. Mutual communication is as taboo as an illegal meeting; lending books, magazines, or manuscripts is considered "circulating anti-state literature." People are ordered to the police station and subjected to humiliating interrogation: what they do, whom they have contacts with, what they think. The police look for "revolutionary literature" in bedrooms, under pillows, and in childrens' toys. On top of that, intellectuals are continually slandered at political meetings and in so-called "scientific" periodicals. Why does all this happen? Let me tell you a few things about historians in Czechoslovakia:

The historians who have been dismissed from the universities, institutes, high schools, and other cultural-historical institutions were not fired because they were poor historians or because there were too many of them, nor were they defeated in a political fight as the regime claims.

If we look at some of the declarations and documents, the reasons for the action are clear: Czechoslovak historians have protested against "a vulgar servitude to a vulgar policy" and have refused to allow any identification of historiography with the politics and ideology practiced by the totalitarian regime. In their daily practice of research, publication, and education, our historians have attempted to continue their long-term fight to emancipate historical science and give it a real social mission. They requested and tried to create conditions for free competition between all Marxist and non-Marxist schools: They insisted on the right of all historians to work scientifically and to publish the results of their research. Even after the tragedy of August 1968 they declared: "We insist on the freedom of scientific research and on unlimited contacts with the scientists of the world. We do not intend to resort to allegories; no theme must be forbidden. And whatever the theme may be, we shall never write in a concealed form." This was written in the declaration of the Historical Institute of the Academy of Science, dated September 25, 1968.

Yet, through the methods I have described, the pens in their hands have been brutally removed, and their works are condemned before they have a chance to defend themselves. In the propaganda campaigns against these historians, pens are turned into daggers, typewriters into machine guns, and books and manuscripts into bombs aimed at the destruction of the foundations of the regime. Many people have been, and still are, accused of "undermining the republic." Up until now, no one has protested this accusation when it was leveled against two of the authors of the above-mentioned Black Book, who did nothing but participate in the compilation and publication of these historical documents.

All this could be seen as merely ridiculous, but we should see the nonsensical rationale of a totalitarian regime that feels threatened by even the smallest enclave of freedom and free thought for the horror that it is. This regime is about to realize the threatening vision of George Orwell: "Who controls the past, controls the future. Who controls the present, controls the past." One might object that, after all, I am an historian and should be able to understand what is happening to my country, to its culture, to my friends and colleagues, and to myself. Or one might say that each country has the right to solve its own problems and consequently this is an "internal affair." If this is true, why am I writing this? There is, finally, the argument that much has already been done, that despite present conditions, human civilization has been saved, its destruction avoided, or at least postponed, and there is nothing more that can be done.

How can these arguments be answered? First of all, to explain something does not mean to agree with it. If a robber attacks me, I know he wants to rob me; when he ties my hands, I know he wants to prevent me from defending myself; if he gags my mouth, I know he wants to stop me from calling for help; if he blindfolds me, I know he does not want me to recognize him. Yet the fact that I know all this does not mean that I am in agreement with him, that I give him the right to do this to me, and that I won't try to defend myself.

It is certainly a great achievement that people have not been destroyed by hydrogen bombs, and that even the era of the Cold War has ended. One can only be pleased that the European Conference on Security proceeds, and any reasonable man will realize that it is inevitable that politicians must accept compromises. This does not mean, however, that blackmail ceases to be blackmail; aggression, aggression; injustice, injustice; and lack of freedom, bondage. Appeasement is terrible in politics, but appeasement in culture leads to its demise, the very negation of itself.

Who has undertaken the mission of searching for the truth about this world and expressing it? Culture—culture in the widest sense of the word including art, literature, science, and all activities that lead to the humanization of the life of the individual, of nations, and of the human community in general. If culture does not intend to destroy itself, it cannot accept compromises that limit the freedom of its own existence, its searching, and its cognitive mission. A living culture means, first and foremost, that people who live without civil rights and freedom to create cannot exist. It is our *right and duty* to defend freedom all over the world, to renew it daily, to deepen it, to re-create it, and to expand its frontiers. And in the context of the rights and duties of human beings toward culture, I protest loudly and openly against the violation of basic human and civil rights in Czechoslovakia.

Furthermore, I protest against the lack of freedom and the destruction of culture, and the persecution of the whole social stratum that is the trustee of culture: writers, artists, researchers in all the branches of science, pedagogues, workers in the field of enlightenment, and all the other creators of culture.

I challenge the right of the Czechoslovak State to treat me as a vassal, to own me as a serf, and to deprive me of my inherent right to validate myself according to my abilities, gifts, interests, and education. In doing so, I demonstrate my desire to realize myself in the field of historical science, wherever it may be in this world, under one condition: that of the freedom of scientific research.

I beg you, dear colleagues, not to deny your solidarity with me in this effort of mine; do not deny me your help. Without this, and I say it quite openly, I have no chance to live in freedom or to work as a historian ever again.

I welcome your Congress, which is also my Congress, and I wish you, and all the historians in the world, all success in our Sisyphean task—to work to know about human beings and the world, its past, and its present.

DR. VILÉM PREČAN
Prague
July 1975

Anna Šabatová (mother of three sentenced children, wife of Dr. Jaroslav Šabata) to all Communist and Workers' Parties

Dear Comrades,

I am writing this letter after much consideration, a few hours after the last member of my family, my twenty-one-year-old daughter, Hana, has been sentenced to three years in prison by the county court in Brno. Like the rest of my family, she will serve without probation.

Perhaps it seems strange that a simple Czechoslovak woman dares to address herself to such high-level institutions as the Central Committees of the Communist and workers' parties of the world. I have done this because at this time in my country of Czechoslovakia, there is no official institution that will listen to me. A letter I wrote in connection with the arrest of my whole family in December of 1971, addressed to Dr. Gustáv Husák, the First Secretary of the Communist Party of Czechoslovakia, has gone unanswered.

I am the mother of three good and beautiful children. Together with my husband I brought them up with great sacrifice. They have taken all of them and put them in prison. Everyone who knew my children liked them and thought highly of them. My youngest son is not even twenty years old. Thus I, as a mother, am in a unique and extraordinary position, and in this, the most painful hour of my life (there was one other, dreadfully bitter moment: August 21, 1968, when the Soviets occupied our country), I do what my duty—my duty as a mother, as a citizen with honor and a long-time conviction that made me work for socialism for twenty-five years, and as a member of the Communist Party of Czechoslovakia—tells me to do.

I am unfortunately aware of all the troubles I will be exposed to because of my frank statement, despite the proclaimed internationalism of my government. I am risking the possibility of imprisonment, but I have nothing to lose. The fact that I may move outside of prison does not mean freedom for me. I cannot even find consolation in my work.

Today, anyone who has been expelled from the Party because he differed from the official judgment of our so-called "international assistants" on August 21, 1968, is forbidden to work anywhere in a responsible position. This refers —as I have been told by official sources—to half a million people. I am not speaking of the other socialists who lost their jobs because of their positive attitude to the democratization of our social life, which was accepted in the spring of 1968 in our Action Program. (At that time the Party made a commitment to the whole nation to fulfill the program.) I myself have been forbidden to continue the job I have held since 1970 in Olomouc, some 70 kilometers from my home. The company, Benzina, in Brno, refused to employ me as a pump attendant.

My husband, a Communist since his nineteenth year, taught at the university in Brno and was, until the fall of 1968, an elected county secretary. After that, he worked in the national enterprise *Inženýrské stavby* (construction industry) up to the time of his imprisonment on November 20. He was sentenced to six and a half years. As a university professor loved by his students, he taught Marxism-Leninism for more than thirteen years and prepared many of his students to become members of the Communist Party. He has been in prison for nine months under conditions that I will not describe in detail out of consideration for the present leadership in Czechoslovakia. I will say that he has had to work very hard despite the warnings of his physicians. (He had a heart attack in 1964 and, as a result of heavy work, is plagued by an inflammation of the mucous membrance of his stomach and a duodenal ulcer.) In

May of 1972 he had a second heart attack. He is given food that makes his stomach ache, despite the fact that I succeeded in getting a certificate from a physician about the state of his health and sent it to the prison.

In this letter I would like to describe at least some of the circumstances of the trials I attended. They were the trial against my sons, Václav and Jan, the trial against seven Communists, all former functionaries of the Party in Brno, and the trial against my daughter. My husband was one of the seven, and it is his trial that I will discuss now.

The court building in which the trial took place was guarded as though a gang of murderers were to be sentenced. The next of kin had to have special permission to wait in the corridor or in front of the entrance to the building. Attempts were made to keep secret many of the trials held during that summer in Prague and Brno, even though they were officially declared open.

You know that foreign correspondents were not admitted, but you may not know that only one near-relative of each of the defendants was allowed to attend these "public" trials. This relative had to apply for a special identity card, which had to be based on his ordinary identity card. It may also be of some interest to you to know that according to our criminal procedures at trials that have been declared non-public because state, military, or economic secrets were involved, each defendant is entitled to name two friends (not more than six altogether) to attend.

The difference between public and secret trials is that a few selected people—representatives of the National Committees and the CPC, but not more than ten altogether—were admitted to the public trials in the summer. Others present were the defendants, their lawyers, the Senate, the prosecutors, the secretary, the uniformed court attendants, State Security agents, police, and the court attendants who escorted the handcuffed prisoners. For the sake of truth, I must add that women defendants were not shackled.

The next of kin, including the defendants' children, could attend only alternately. In Brno, two relatives of a defendant were not permitted to attend the trial at the same time. On the formal side the Senate acted according to the rules, and the defendants were permitted to say whatever they considered important.

All of the defendants were sincere adherents of socialism. All of them were described by their neighbors and colleagues as active citizens who were known to have helped build the socialist state with great personal sacrifice. In the trial against the seven Communists (six were county secretaries, one, a district secretary), the president of the Senate stated while explaining the sentence: "Neither the Senate as a whole nor any of its members came to the conclusion that the sentenced were enemies of socialism." These Communists were sentenced because their views differed from the official ones and because they expressed their opinions orally or in writing, to each other or within a small circle of people whom the defendants had known for some time through their Party activities or in their work. To be as precise as possible, the defendants had distributed magazines published abroad; magazines such as *Listy** or material from various foreign Communist publications. Among the prosecutor's evidence was a leaflet about the extraordinary Fourteenth Party Congress of the CPC which was published not in Czechoslovakia but by the Communist Party in Italy. My husband had also worked on some theoretical material, the Little Action Program, for example, which was meant as a basis for discussion. In the program he tried to formulate a common platform for Communist and non-Marxist socialists who held a positive attitude toward a socialist order in Czechoslovakia.

I would like to emphasize that the Little Action Program explicitly states that nationalization was a necessary and just act and that it should not be altered. It is not true that my husband or any of the defendants were adherents of bourgeois democracy; they were all unequivocal supporters of socialist democracy. My husband always put emphasis on control from below, i.e., on the will of the people.

*Published by the Czech socialist opposition in Rome.

I believe that a number of Communist and other leftist-oriented trade-union organizations, as well as the world public, are right to be disturbed by these trials. I am convinced that the Communist and workers' parties, individual Communists and Marxists, and all other friends of socialism have the right to express their views on these trials of Communists, socialists, and other citizens.

The international Communist and workers' movement must find a common language, one based on the actuality as well as the appearance of events in Czechoslovakia. In this context, I would ask the following questions: Why is the night attack of allied armies against Czechoslovakia regarded as international help, and the disapproval of it by many Communist and leftist parties considered interference in our internal affairs? Why are Czechoslovak citizens not informed by the official Czechoslovak press about this critical attitude? And one more question: Why were these trials kept secret?

It is worth mentioning that the investigation against my sons was closed on March 2, 1972, while the trial took place at the end of July during the long summer vacation. Thus, the detention pending the investigation was prolonged for four months in the trial of my sons, while the trial against my husband took place only three days after the investigation was finished.

One last point: To change the tragic fate of sentenced Czechoslovak citizens it is not enough to protest to Communist and anti-imperialist institutions. I am deeply convinced that what is needed—today, more than ever—is to work on a clarification of theoretical-political questions at the highest level within the Communist movement itself. The most important issue in question is how to deal with the power that the victory of the working class has gained. In my view it is not logical that only those who are ruling their countries should speak, because it is the working class itself that holds the power.

It is important to give perspectives to the Communist parties and their allies in countries where the bourgeoisie still reigns. Socialism should be attractive to all strata of society. One needs allies, not only in the period of the fight for power and the first years of building socialism but, in the interest of the Communist world movement, also later, in the period of a developed socialist society. We must have the support of all democrats, and democratic rights must be truly valid, not simply formally accepted.

Anna Šabatová

Zdeněk Mlynář to the Communists and Socialists of Europe

With this personal letter I address myself to my comrades and friends in the Communist and socialist parties in Europe in the hope that I can, at least to some degree, contribute to the solution of some of the most important problems facing my country. Without the help of the European workers' movement, I don't see how these problems can be solved.

Eight years ago, in August 1968, a very different letter was mailed from Czechoslovakia. It was addressed to only a small group of Communist parties, and its authors were ashamed to sign it. The text of this letter was published by the Soviet paper *Pravda,* on August 22, to show why five nations of the Warsaw Pact sent their armies into Czechoslovakia and occupied her territories. This letter was supposed to prove that these events occurred because responsible and influential Czechoslovak personalities had asked for help. To this day it is not known who these people were.

Nevertheless, the leadership of the CPC and its foreign protectors have defended the right to write such a letter and have even seen it as an act of Communist internationalism. Therefore, I hope that our political representatives will not object if I myself write a personal letter and express my views about the political situation in Czechoslovakia to my friends in the Communist and socialist parties in Europe. I will not even ask them to send their armies in support of my views, and on top of that, I will even sign the letter.

In the framework of the strategy of the world powers, the Czechoslovak problem has a local and internal political character; it will not trigger a conflict between the great nations of the world. However, in the European Communist and socialist movements this problem is certainly not one of simply internal affairs or of a local character, and I am convinced that some of the political concepts applied by the official state power of my country not only do great damage to the development of Czechoslovakia but also represent a serious threat to the prospects of socialist development throughout Europe.

In Europe we see two kinds of nations existing next to each other: those that have eliminated the economic and political power of capital and the bourgeoisie, where Communist parties rule and realize programs in the building of socialism and Communism; and countries where the power of capital, monopolies, and the bourgeoisie is an undisputed fact. In this situation the prospects for socialist development can be undermined not only by the attempts of the capitalists to prevent the working class from becoming the rulers of society but also when the vital problems of the liberation of the working people—in countries where socialism and Communism are already being built—are not solved in ways that are attractive to the working classes of other countries.

The prospects for a socialist Europe, a Europe without the dictates of capitalist monopolies and imperialist arbitrariness, are an essential part of the overall socialist program. After a long effort a common political platform has now been formulated at the Helsinki Conference, in the Final Act for Security and Cooperation in Europe, and this could turn out to be the political framework for the further development of European nations. It is in the interest of all nations, and of the working classes throughout Europe, to see this platform as more than a tactical maneuver in power politics. The European workers' movement, Communists and socialists alike, should adopt binding decisions for their own policies from it. A socialist Europe that respects the sovereignty of individual countries without applying force in international relations can exist in peacetime if democratic principles and political freedom for all citizens of all nations are maintained. These rights and freedoms are an integral part of the traditions of European civilization, out of which the socialist and Communist movements emerged.

At a time when the further development of socialism is not linked to war, a military bloc can no longer be regarded as the germinating force. The existence of military and political blocs is the result of conditions that can be overcome by applying the political ideals of the Helsinki Conference. In the future it will no longer be possible to divide Europe into a capitalist and a socialist sector and to describe it in terms of politico-military blocs. The germinating forces of socialism are the socialist forces in every country, and the international goals of socialism can be achieved only when these forces are supported and united. This must become the main task of the present European workers' movement.

Similarly, Communist and socialist leaderships must respect the basic democratic rights and political freedom of their citizens. Socialism must establish itself and develop under European conditions as a social system that guarantees more than any bourgeois democracy. This contradicts the concept that formal democratic rights and freedoms are meaningless where "the People reign." The critics of the Twentieth Party Congress of the Soviet Union revealed that such a concept was used by Stalin to deprive people of their most basic human rights, to violate laws, and to make use of brutal forces against socialist society. Thus, it is not only the political platform of the Helsinki Conference but also the actual experience of the Communist parties that should lead us to extinguish such demagoguery from European workers' parties once and for all.

The importance of political democracy has come further and further into the foreground in Europe today as peace and cooperation among nations have been consolidated, and this process will eventually undermine reactionary and dictatorial regimes. The end of the military-fascist dictatorships in Greece and Portugal and the growing hope of a democracy in Spain are all proof that the last remnants of fascism in Europe are disappearing. The policy of freedom and cooperation also diminishes the danger of open intervention (particularly military intervention) by capitalist countries to prevent socialism.

European socialists can therefore no longer underestimate

the importance of the development of political democracy. In fact, the real growth of socialism is possible only in connection with such a development. For the workers' movement it must become not an end in itself but a means to realize far-reaching social changes and to introduce socialist relationships into the economy and social life. This is the only way to bring about the further development in countries where capitalism has been eliminated. Socialism, combined with political democracy, will finally lead to the participation of the working population in the decisions, control, and administration of the society, to a true self-government by the workers. Thus, political democracy is of great value to the workers' movement. It cannot be limited or oppressed for the sake of higher forms of democracy, because the higher forms integrate the rights and freedoms of the bourgeoisie. I believe that this is the true meaning of the political endeavors of the most important Communist parties in Western Europe.

It is, of course, understandable that under these conditions the crucial question of the European workers' movement again comes to the fore: Is not merely a tactical but a real cooperation between Communists and socialists possible and desirable? The open hostility and sharp differences between the two groups have their roots in conditions that have prevailed in Europe over the past fifty years; new conditions will necessarily create new possibilities. Even today there are differences in the workers' movement in regard to a number of problems in the social transformation of society, but these should not be insurmountable obstacles to effective cooperation between socialist, Communists, and other leftist groups as well. If the political participants fully respect the autonomy of each group, they will respect the rules of political democracy as well. If this cooperation takes place, there will be no room for either the socialists' reactionary policy of banning the Communist Party, or the Communists' sectarian political logic that sees only temporary allies in non-Communist, socialist groups, the independent political existence of which they plan to ban after the victory has been achieved.

A number of political documents and statements by European socialist and Communist parties, as well as discussions within the workers' movement, prove that even within the Communist movement there are still many problems. Only after these problems are solved will it be possible for the Communist movement to concentrate in a politically serious and responsible way on the task of developing socialism under conditions of peace and cooperation in Europe. If the socialist forces in each country are recognized as the decisive, drawing force, then each country's socialist party must be guaranteed full autonomy and independence. The unity of Communist parties must be understood as a democratic unity. This presupposes the existence of disagreements and precludes the oppression of minority views.

The European Communist movement can achieve this unity only in a democratic way. Any attempt to create an enforced, pseudo-unity and the suppression of real disagreements will merely hurt the interests of the movement in the long run. In addition, democratic relationships must be introduced between individual Communist parties and between those who reign and those who have not yet succeeded in participating in the state-power. It is be understood that Communist parties in all countries will support countries where a socialist revolution has taken place and where the Communist Party rules. However, such support does not exclude criticism when the policy of the ruling party is wrong or unacceptable. The fact that a Communist Party has a power monopoly does not mean that it has a monopoly on truth; nor does it mean that it has the right to suppress the critics of other parties. The assumption that only the Communists in power represent the "real socialism" is wrong and anti-Marxist. It is an expression of the uncritical self-confidence of a monopolistic ruler.

If socialist and Communist goals are not mere theoretical postulates but authentic political practices, they must be approached by each party in a specific way, according to the historical (and consequently special) conditions of individual political actions. No single party can be the embodiment of laws valid for all other parties. The political actions and experiences of individual parties can be democratically accepted by other parties only when, based on their own analysis, they come to the conclusion that these experiences are useful for them and in harmony with the attempts of the working class of that particular country. Furthermore, those who criticize representatives of their own party—declare them to be renegades and traitors or even attempt to exclude them from the Communist movement simply because they do not accept and follow political methods applied elsewhere—have already done great harm to the development of socialism and have contributed to its defeat in some countries. This was Stalin's logic. He forced acceptance of his methods by the whole Communist movement.

The present conditions in Czechoslovakia are the fruits of this catastrophic political approach. The CPC has been condemned because of its attempts to democratize its socialist system in 1968. This policy was part of the revolutionary efforts of the CPC after the war to respect the democratic traditions and goals of the Czechoslovak people while building a socialist order, and it was thanks to this policy that a great majority of the population supported the Party. This was so obvious that even the authors of the request for military intervention in 1968 wrote: "The basic rights of citizens, which have always been tied to democracy and humanism in the minds of our people, were revived in the progressive spirit of the Action Program. This long-term platform of our socialist development achieved extraordinarily massive support by our people."

But the leadership of certain other Communist parties regarded the political developments of 1968 as undesirable, and the CPC was forced to accept different and, in fact, opposing political views. In 1970, under the "exchange of Party cards," the CPC was literally dashed to pieces. The decisive questions in the exchange were: who had abandoned the ideals of the Action Program, and who had not; who was or was not willing to recognize military intervention as "a brotherly attempt to help save socialism from counterrevolution." Approximately half a million members of the CPC (something like one-third of all its members) were expelled from the Party and stigmatized as "anti-socialist and anti-Soviet forces," "agents of the counterrevolution," and so on. The officials of the trade unions were treated in the same manner, even though these were the largest organizations of the working class as far as membership was concerned. Hundreds of thousands of citizens who were not members of the Party but who were convinced that the democratic reforms of 1968 were correct were similarly stigmatized.

In present-day Czechoslovakia the problem is not the so-called "dissidents" or the fact that some individuals express criticism and displeasure at the silencing of different groups in the society. The real problem is that hundreds of thousands of individuals who have represented a certain stream of thought in European Communism and democratic movements for years are being persecuted, oppressed, and silenced. This stream of thought is often identical to that of groups who have recently become increasingly active in the European workers' movement, as is particularly clear in the political development of the Communist parties in Italy, Sweden, Belgium, and some other countries. Their views are also similar to that of the Yugoslav Communists and, in some respects, to the Rumanians as well.

At this point I should say that my letter is of course a personal one, and no one in Czechoslovakia who has similar views is in a position to hear them echoed in the nation, as their publication is prohibited. In addition, I would hope that these and other views of mine would be critically discussed, as they are not at all binding on those who are attempting to further democratic development in Czechoslovakia. Nevertheless, I think that one would be correct in assuming that the ideas about the basic questions concerning the prospects for socialist development in Europe briefly formulated here are not simply those of a few individuals. Actually, they are characteristic of the wide range of ideas of both Communists and socialists that have been silenced in Czechoslovakia. Let the European Communist and socialist parties judge whether or not these views are "anti-socialist and counterrevolutionary."

A number of documents have been published abroad; the most important facts about the persecution of Communists and socialists whose views differ from the official ones are well known. These people are "sentenced" to forced labor without court action and with no consideration for their abilities and qualifications; the work they are required to perform needs no special talent. The same applies to members of their families; their children, for example, are not permitted to attend high schools, trade schools or universities. The views of these people may not be published, and even an attempt to do so is threatened with imprisonment.

Many of them have been in prison for years. Anyone who is suspected of thinking differently from the Party line, anyone who writes down his views or attempts to communicate with his friends about them is subject to persecution by the secret police. His freedom is curtailed, his human contacts and friendships destroyed; he is not permitted to travel abroad or to work at certain types of jobs. European socialists and Communists can easily confirm these facts simply by getting in touch with official institutions or by direct contact with those persecuted, silenced, and isolated from the international workers' movement.

What is the actual difference between this state of affairs and that brought about by the Stalinist methods unanimously rejected at the XXth Party Congress? Basically, the only difference is that there are no executions and the number of political prisoners is much smaller. Stalinist logic is not only being preserved in Czechoslovakia, it is being systematically and consciously extended.

The signatures of the highest representatives of Czechoslovakia on the Final Act of the Helsinki Conference have made only one difference for those who have "oppositionist" views: before, they were called "anti-socialists" and "counterrevolutionaries;" now, after the Helsinki Conference, they are called "warmongers." Thus, for example, the official publication of the CPC, *Rudé právo*, on January 4, 1976, printed a story about the different renegades who "serve bourgeois, anti-Soviet and anti-peace propaganda," citing "pamphlets, articles, and statements by Dubček, Mlynař, Kriegel, and some other people living in Czechoslovakia whose hatred for the social and political order is boiling over." Yet none of the letters, statements, or articles attacked by *Rudé právo* are in contradiction to the content of this letter.

No doubt, anyone outside of the Warsaw Pact countries may read the texts *Rudé právo* has in mind. And if they do, and want to characterize these letters with the word "anti-," they must call them "anti-" Stalinist. I must ask whether it is possible to identify Stalin's concepts and methods with Communism and socialism in 1976? This is a crucial question, and one that transcends the internal politics of Czechoslovakia today. All European socialists have not only the right but the duty to answer this question clearly and unequivocally.

Exactly twenty years ago Stalinism was condemned at the XXth Party Congress. Since that time, a battle has been waged within all Communist parties, whether they are ruling parties or not, between those who want to overcome Stalinism and those who verbally oppose it but, in their political practice, try to apply its logic and methods. This conflict, particularly in the ruling parties, is not always visible, but it exists and is as yet unresolved. The political line of the peace initiative by the Soviet Union and the spirit of Helsinki are the result of tendencies toward overcoming the Stalinist heritage. Yet at the same time other forces are trying, both ideologically and politically, to interpret this policy in their own way. Often we can see the conflict between these two orientations in the policies of a single party or in the ideas of a single party representative.

Today in Czechoslovakia a special situation prevails. The overwhelming majority of Communists who fought against the Stalinist heritage within the Party, and who succeeded in bringing about a policy of democratization in 1968, have not only been expelled from the Party but are considered virtual outlaws. They are trapped in a ghetto in which they have no rights; they have become citizens without the privileges of citizenship. Their demands for the application of the political principles of Helsinki in Czechoslovakia have been declared voices of "anti-socialist elements and appeals to interference with internal affairs," activities "against the spirit of Helsinki" that provoke war. This is nothing but an example of Stalinist demagoguery!

It is a pretense to declare that a position that ties political democracy with socialism is interference in "internal affairs" and to have it outlawed, despite the fact that in the European workers' movement this position represents a positive guarantee of primary importance for the further development of European socialism. Let other Communist and socialist parties decide whether or not this situation is their concern—whether it is an internal affair concerning only the leadership of the CPC or just the opposite, a political line harmful to the interests of European socialism.

There is an obvious reactionary tendency in Europe that considers the Helsinki platform unrealistic and naïve. It is not my purpose to describe in detail the danger of the capitalist, monopolist circles hidden behind such tendencies. In the context of this letter it is important to notice that these tendencies can always be found where the anachronistic remnants of Stalinist concepts and methodology appear in the political practices of the workers' movement.

The Czechoslovak former first secretary of the Communist Party has been accused of being an "anti-Communist" whose "hatred" for socialism "boils over" and who is assisting the advocates of the Cold War. However, the only "crime" he committed was that of having a critical attitude toward the dictatorial methods of his followers. If this is possible, what can we call those who have never been Communists, or even socialists, but who stand for freedom and democracy in Europe? What will a regime do with these people if it persecutes confirmed Communists and their children, men and women who fought for the Party for over a quarter of a century, who have different views than those of the official leadership? It is realistic to assume that such a regime understands Helsinki only as a political maneuver and uses the verbal recognition of democratic rights and freedom merely as a fig leaf to cover the sensitive spots of a dictatorship. These are very impressive arguments for those who would like to bury the political platform of Helsinki as an unrealistic illusion.

I am deeply convinced that if the European socialist movement is really interested in realizing the potential offered by the Helsinki Conference, it must help to establish political democracy in Czechoslovakia. In 1968 a brief period of democratic socialism was achieved with the help of inner forces. In the period of only a few months, this policy of democratization enjoyed such popularity that it was impossible to suppress it without military intervention. This should be remembered, particularly by those who are afraid of supporting the silenced and oppressed Czechoslovak Communists, socialists, and democrats because they might be accused of interfering with the nation's internal affairs.

If the inner forces of our country were again given the opportunity to choose the political orientation of Czechoslovakia democratically, the present retarding influence would be replaced by one of the most active political forces in the strengthening of socialist influence and of policies of peace and cooperation in Europe. European Communists could be of great help in this endeavor if they would say "no" to the attempts to stigmatize Czechoslovak Communists and socialists as "anti-socialist forces" and to negate the fact that we belong to the European Communist and socialist movements.

If this letter serves as an impetus for at least a few of the participants in the revolutionary European workers' movement to look earnestly for ways of contributing to the achievement of their goals, it has accomplished its task.

ZDENĚK MLYNÁŘ
Prague
February 1968

An Open Letter from Various Czechoslovak Writers to Heinrich Böll

Dear Heinrich Böll,

On August 20 a trial will take place in our country that is both absurd and, for these times, unique: Fourteen young people will be tried, not because of their political views, activities, or demands, but because of their attitudes toward life. These youths, whose musical productions and literary texts have had an important share in forming a specific, underground culture, committed a "crime." This "crime" consisted of writing and performing songs and compositions that expressed their unwillingness to accept the values and morals of their environment, and their rebellion against the uniformity of life, bureaucratic stupidity, and consumerism in their country; they refused to be corrupted by the temptations the establishment offered them. In a world of conformity and hypocrisy, they dared to acknowledge their individuality and to express their zeal for life by their performances.

Naturally, none of this can be read in the indictment: there we read only about the "excesses" and vulgar expressions in their allegedly offensive songs. The senselessness of these accusations is underlined by the fact that, among other things, the defendants never performed publicly; this was forbidden years ago. They sang only at private, legal occasions (such as weddings), to which they had been invited by their friends. Yet thanks to these absurd accusations they are now threatened with a rather extreme punishment. This threat is real; some of their friends—three young workers—were sentenced to prison a short time ago for having helped to organize the defendants' shows. Also, if the trial itself is any indication, it should be mentioned that public attendance has been banned.

It is paradoxical that only a year after Helsinki, and some years since the reinforcement of its power, the establishment feels threatened by people who sing a few songs in private; not even the indictment mentions a hostile political attitude. What will be the result of public acceptance of this action? Who will feel safe from persecution for similar absurd accusations?

You have often, dear Heinrich Böll, expressed your concern for Czechoslovak culture; your voice has often defended those who were oppressed in this country because of their views, attitudes, and creativity. This is the reason we address you. We beg you with all our hearts to make use of your authority as an artist and a human being and appeal to the Czechoslovak authorities to stop this tragic mockery of justice. You can awaken the interest of other prominent figures who are concerned with the fate of culture and of freedom of spirit on our continent. We ask you this because our own voices are not heard: No one has answered us; both our private appeals to the President of the republic and the declarations we have sent to the mass media, which were published abroad, have been ignored.

You know that freedom is indivisible, the more so since it is threatened and persecuted everywhere. Because of this, solidarity, which transcends not only the boundaries of individual spheres of creativity but also the boundaries of state and of social systems, has a deep justification. The defendants, Ivan Jirous, Svatopluk Karásek, Karel Soukup, and the other imprisoned young men are not known abroad and are therefore easily persecuted. This is why it is so important to gain the support of the European public. We feel strongly about this because to us, the harsh punishment given to these youths as our "proxies" is possible only because they do not enjoy the support of their colleagues abroad. Though we are working in different cultural and spiritual fields, we cannot accept the status of some prominent "protected species," and allow others, less protected than ourselves, to be sentenced as criminals without the attention of the world.

We beg you to use your influence for the sake of these young people about to be tried.

> With friendly greetings,
> JAROSLAV SEIFERT, poet, national artist
> PROF. VÁCLAV ČERNY, literary historian
> PROF. JAN PATOČKA, philosopher
> PROF. KAREL KOSÍK, philosopher
> VÁCLAV HAVEL, writer
> IVAN KLÍMA, writer
> PAVEL KOHOUT, writer
> Prague
> *August 1976*

Heinrich Böll
to Jaroslav Seifert

Dear Jaroslav Seifert,

When your letter came, I was reading Reiner Kunze's book, *The Wonderful Years,* for the second time. I read it with growing horror, and what you and your friends have told me seemed to illustrate the book, as its topic is the "wonderful years" of the rising generation, not of the adults.

Your letter described a desperate state of affairs, more absurd than one could possibly imagine. However, in spite of this I found solace in your letter: I don't know of any other group of poets, philosophers, or professors in any socialist country that would have addressed itself to the public outside its country (it is assumed that it could not address itself to its own nation, having no access to the media) in favor of unknown youths whose crime was to sing songs and make music.

What impressed me most was the fact that you refuse to be what you called a "protected species," to capitalize on that aura of prominence used everywhere in the world as a smoke screen for problems. This problem is as international as the attempts to intimidate young people, to stop them, to deprive them of their rights of free expression, to make them take oaths (regularly) in support of a reactionary image of a society without conflicts, with prescribed thoughts, prescibed music and literature, and prescribed behavior.

I cannot judge whether the trial was postponed simply because the authorities suddenly realized that nothing could be more ridiculous than to allow it to take place. For those concerned, however, it is not at all "ridiculous," for even if this trial is never held, the threat of similar incidents remains.

To you and your friends who signed your letter, my most heartfelt thanks, especially because, aside from your information about the trial, your concept of the "protected species," which you and your friends refuse to accept, has added a new dimension to the "cultural scene." We here in Germany also have reason to regard our "protected area" with great suspicion. This is a matter of course, like the expression of close ties you so heartily emphasized.

I thank you for your letter. My friends accept it as being addressed to them as well, and when I offer you and your colleagues greetings from the bottom of my heart, may I also enclose the greetings of many of them. With sincere greetings to the young musicians as well,

Yours,
HEINRICH BÖLL
Köln
September 4, 1976

Pavel Kohout:
His Own Position

On May 15, 1976, I made an application to the passport division of the Ministry of the Interior to obtain permission to travel to the premiere of my play, *Poor Murderer,* on Broadway. The invitation to come to New York stated explicitly that all costs—travel and accommodation expenses—would be paid for by the German publisher and the American producer. After ninety days my application was refused with the explanation that it is "not in the interest of Czechoslovakia to permit travel abroad for which foreign currency is not available."

On September 29 I appealed this decision (according to the rules of the very office which forbade the trip), proving that the logic behind this decision did not correspond to the reality of the situation. Up to now I have not received a reply.

On August 24 and September 3, 20, and 23, I sent the Minister of the Interior letters, explaining politely and in a matter-of-fact fashion why I felt that my application was just and that its rejection was in contradiction to the law. I have asked Minister Obzina five times to grant me an appointment for a few minutes in order to try to work out a compromise solution. All of these letters were answered in a single sentence by the Office of the Minister stating that my letter "will be dealt with by competent organs."

On this occasion I must make the following remarks:

In the Czechoslovak mass media it is all too often declared an interference in our internal affairs if a foreign theater decides to present the play of an author who is not "officially" recommended (because his plays are forbidden here). This creates the impression that the plays my colleagues and I write are performed abroad only as a reward for our anti-socialist activities, perhaps even out of funds provided by foreign intelligence agencies. This is not only an offense against the more than two hundred theaters that have put on more than five thousand performances of my plays, but also an act of violence. The Ministry of Culture appropriates artistic creations and then "expropriates" the people to whom they belong: the audiences and readers at home.

This situation has lasted for seven years and is becoming more dangerous as the causes continue to be hidden. In 1968 I was accused of an alleged crime; today I am stigmatized in the press, radio, and in hundreds of mass meetings, as someone who has attacked socialism since childhood and even today makes use of every opportunity to defame the socialist system and his own country. Therefore, I must declare:

1. Before 1968 I did not do or say anything different from what all Communists critical of the offenses against the law in the fifties (or of Novotný's police and bureaucratic regime) did or said. Many leading politicians of the present regime have done and said the same things.

2. After August of 1968 my reactions were within the framework of the state and Party documents. I did not then, and do not now agree that they were later voided, but regardless of this, I have committed no acts that would justify the government's persecution of me, which has continued since 1969.

3. Beginning in 1969 I requested—with no success whatsoever—answers to dozens of letters. In these letters I offered much proof that my persecution violated our laws and, in particular, that it was based on verbal instructions or secret orders.

4. My petitions and rebuttals in the foreign press, where I defended myself against lies because I had no other means to do so, have been declared to be concrete acts of hostility.

5. In the fall of 1975, immediately after Helsinki, I was permitted, for the first time in six years, to travel abroad on three occasions. With the permission to travel abroad, the ab-

surd accusations of the past against me were, *via facti,* voided. However, my hopes that this was the first step in a gradual, rational solution to my problems were not fulfilled. For the past two years at least I have been offered risky and humiliating opportunities to leave the country; I have not taken them. In Czechoslovakia any thief or criminal is regarded as a citizen with full rights after he has served his time in prison; he is far better off than I, who have been waiting for seven years and may have to wait until the end of my life for a concrete accusation. Yet even without it, I have been and continue to be punished.

I have asked my government to investigate my case and bring it to an end. If the prosecutor has evidence that I acted against the law in 1968 or before, let him show it, prove my guilt, and indict me. If not, the Ministries of the Interior and Culture, as well as other institutions, should end their sanctions, which have put me in an apartheid situation since 1969. This is in contradiction to our own Constitution as well as to the Charter on Human Rights, not to mention the Final Act on Security and Cooperation in Europe, which, although signed by our President, has been turned into a worthless piece of paper.

My life's work is proof that I am a socialist; I have definite views, but no ambition for power. I am a writer, and I am trying to find the truth and oppose the misuse of power wherever it appears.

I am not the one who is looking for new confrontations, and I do not ask that the powers that be love me. I do ask, however, that they allow me to do my everyday work and to live my life in a normal way.

Appendix

Charter '77: Documents Nos. 2–10

CHARTER '77: DOCUMENT NO. 2

On the morning of January 6, 1972, in the midst of normal traffic, a car containing the writers Václav Havel and Ludvík Vaculík and the actor Pavel Landovský was surrounded by cars operated by members of the State Security. These three men were on their way to present the signed text of Charter '77 to the government, the Parliament, and the news agency CTK, and to mail the Charter to all of its co-signers. Some of the co-signers, including Zdeněk Urbánek, were interrogated for many hours. This action by the State Security forces was unjustified; as experts in the law can prove, Charter '77 does not violate Czechoslovak laws—rather, it advocates their fulfillment.

The apparatus of the Ministry of the Interior has—not for the first time—ignored international agreements, as well as our own laws. Dozens of cars participated in this action against citizens of good reputation, and an army of agents, technicians, and supervisors was either present or behind the scenes, as if to prevent one of our recent hijackings. During the interrogation those arrested were filmed by television cameras and photographed, along with the confiscated documents addressed to our highest representatives, as if they had been spies. The State Security agents also photographed the apartment and country house of Václav Havel, despite his protests, and Urbánek's apartment as well. Collections of foreign publications and different personal objects, laid out as if they had been the weapons of a terrorist, were also photographed.

During the nights of January 6 and 7, and the following day, the homes of those named were searched, and books, correspondence, photographs, and many other personal items were confiscated. Like the articles confiscated during the searches of April 1975, much that was taken will be used for blackmail purposes. Hence, Item No. 1 on the list of items confiscated from Ludvík Vaculík was the book *Group Portrait With Lady,* by Heinrich Böll, although the rest of the list is not so detailed; one item farther down, for instance, was "Sixty hardbound manuscripts." For the second time they confiscated the manuscript of a novel Vaculík had only begun to write. Official publications of the American embassy in Prague were taken and filmed. It is worth mentioning that the collection of texts containing the laws of the Helsinki Agreement on the rights of citizens were also taken.

At the same time the writer František Pávliček and the journalist Jan Petránek, both signers of the Charter, were arrested and interrogated. While the first four were released after midnight on January 7 along with Václav Havel (after his second arrest the same day at 10 P.M.), the other two men were not released until a day later.

With these measures the State Security Agency established Charter '77's right to exist, by definitely violating citizen's rights. The Charter pointed out to the Ministry of the Interior that the searches violated the law because the prosecutor hadn't had a search warrant. To film people against their will is coercion, according to paragraph 237 of the Penal Code, as is the filming of their apartments and their property. During the entire incident, the authors of Charter '77 and other co-signers protested against this arbitrary action; they are now requesting the cessation of further lawlessness, and the immediate return of the confiscated documents and property.

The authors of Charter '77 reserve the right, according to paragraph 19 of the International Agreement concerning political and citizens' rights, to publicize any improper pressure on the co-signers or other citizens. They further declare that the

Ministry of the Interior made it impossible for them to deliver
the Charter to the respective organs of the government and is
consequently responsible for the text's publication abroad before it could be presented to the Czechoslovak authorities.

The authors of Charter '77 would like to announce that
forty new signatures have been added, although the names will
not be published until a guarantee is made that the police action
of January 6 will not be repeated. Nevertheless, the new co-
signers will participate in the work of the Charter.

The authors of Charter '77 further declare that they have
appointed three deputies, whose names will be made public
when the first three authors are no longer able to fulfill their
duties.

The speakers of Charter '77 appreciate expressions of solidarity, both in our country and abroad, and wish to correct
some statements being made that all the co-signers are intellectuals. Actually, workers and other employed citizens also signed
Charter '77, and people who were not even exposed to the
repression stemming from the events of 1969 are among them.
For these reasons the signers of the Charter "should not be seen
as a group of dissidents, but as the result of citizens' initiative."

The speakers of Charter '77 believe that our leading statesmen will prohibit further arbitrary action by the Ministry of the
Interior. Such actions endanger not only many citizens but—as
the past has shown—the initiators of these incidents as well.

This manifesto is signed by the authors of Charter '77:

PROF. JAN PATOČKA
VÁCLAV HAVEL
PROF. JIŘÍ HÁJEK
Prague
January 8, 1977

CHARTER '77: DOCUMENT NO. 3

To the Praesidium of the Federal Parliament of Czechoslovakia
To the Praesidium of the Czechoslovak Government
To the News Agency CTK

In the declaration of Charter '77, 242 citizens addressed themselves to the highest offices of the state and to the general public, announcing that they had decided to attempt to realize the standards of the International Agreement on Human Rights. These standards fell under the jurisdiction of the general population when they were published in the Collection of Laws of Czechoslovakia under No. 120/76. This is in accordance with Articles 28 and 29 of the Constitution of Czechoslovakia, as well as with Article 19 of the International Agreement on Citizens' and Political Rights.

On January 6, agents of the State Security arrested citizens who were about to personally present the Charter documents, with authentic signatures, to the highest offices in Czechoslovakia. The documents were confiscated and consequently had to be mailed to these offices. To date the only response has been far-reaching repression by the State Security agencies and a slanderous campaign against the co-signers of the Charter by the mass media. This vicious propaganda campaign can be compared only to the campaign during the years of the unlawful political trials. As happened at that time, campaigns have been organized in shops, factories, schools, and other institutions to make the citizenry—either as groups or as individuals—condemn something they have no information about. Signatures are required on forms condemning Charter '77, and refusal to sign can endanger one's livelihood; in some places these forms are presented as ultimatums accompanying wage and salary payments. Yet the text of the Charter has not been published and, as *Rudé právo* wrote on January 15, it will never be published.

During the night of Thursday, January 13, 1977, many of the co-signers were taken to police headquarters and, although they had been brought in only as witnesses, searches of some of their homes were made. They were picked up by the police between four and five o'clock in the morning for no apparent reason, and many were treated roughly, as if they were potential criminals.

Almost every day for a week the authors of Charter '77 were interrogated and released only at night. On January 13, after a search of his home, the journalist Jiří Lederer was arrested, and on the 14th one of the authors, the writer Václav Havel, was taken in for interrogation and never returned. A phone call from his wife on the morning of January 15 was answered with the explanation that "Václav Havel succumbed to the police" and was being kept for reasons not connected with the Charter. Also on January 13, the university lecturers F. Jiránek and Dr. R. Palouš were fired. The decision was made by the Collegium of the University simply because they had signed Charter '77. The same treatment is being prepared for many others.

We believe that this is sufficient proof of how urgent it is to find solutions to the problems of our country in accordance with the instituting of human rights, which the government is internationally obligated to respect. The declaration of the Charter explicitly states—and we repeat it here—that the aim of this undertaking by the citizens of this nation is not to promote political activism.

The campaign against Charter '77 consists primarily of political propaganda; the terms "counterrevolutionary" and "anti-socialist" are used repeatedly to describe our aims. From this campaign we can assume that the government regards respect for citizens' rights to be dangerous to its own interests, even though it has committed itself to the guarantee of these rights. We believe that it is up to the political parties, trade unions, and similar organizations throughout Europe to judge whether or not this kind of respect is, in fact, "anti-socialist," "anti-human," or even "counterrevolutionary." The co-signers of Charter '77 feel that their judgment would be in our favor.

Out of responsibility as the authors of Charter '77 we request:

1. that the police repression against the co-signers of Charter '77 be stopped;
2. that all citizens who were arrested in connection with the declarations of Charter '77 be released;
3. that the blackmail, particularly that which threatens the livelihoods of citizens who are only asking for the human rights specified in the International Agreement, be eliminated;

4. and that the Czechoslovak public be informed about the content and declarations of Charter '77.

In addition, we ask that the organs of political power start to consider how the problem of application of citizens' rights can be solved in Czechoslovakia.

We are willing and prepared to help with these considerations.

PROF. JAN PATOČKA
PROF. JIŘÍ HÁJEK
Prague
January 15, 1977

CHARTER '77: DOCUMENT NO. 4

The discrimination against young people that is practiced in the selection of applicants for study at high schools and universities has been a burning issue of human rights for many years. Each year a great number of youths are deprived of the opportunity to study, despite the fact that their grades, character, interest in further study, and achievement in the entrance examinations are proof of their qualifications. It is a form of discrimination that has lasted for too long and has affected many different people. The rules are not published but are strictly adhered to and produce great inconvenience for Czechs and Slovaks alike. Though the measures are unlawful, they are effective in depriving people of a number of human rights, among them their children's right to an education. Earlier, the families that were affected were the so-called kulaks (landowners), the families of political prisoners or of soldiers who served in the Western armies during the Second World War, the families of emigrants, the families that practiced one religion or another, etc. Today, it is applied to the families of citizens who were engaged in public, political, scientific, or artistic activities in 1968.

The accusations against these citizens are not at all objective. Today, a large part of the international Communist and workers' movement accepts the democratic principles for which these people fought and which the government of Czechoslovakia supported in 1968, the same government in which the current President, Dr. Gustáv Husák, and a government official, Dr. Lubomír Štrougal, were deputy prime ministers. The supporters of these democratic principles could not be indicted and tried, and so the discrimination against them is a matter of arbitrary action, often a matter of settling personal accounts. Yet even if they could be sentenced according to law, the punishment cannot be extended to innocent people, especially to children. The punishment of children in a most sensitive field—the field of education, the preparation for their future—is therefore unlawful. It also contradicts any definition of a normal, humane society, especially of a society that declares itself to be socialist.

It is an act of revenge, intimidation, and corruption against parents, teachers, and children—young people, about to prepare themselves for life, who could become the willing supporters of the state.

Eight years after "normalization" was declared, children who were only seven or eight years old in 1968 are not permitted to attend high school if their parents supported the democratization of our public and political life, and children who were only ten or eleven are not permitted to attend universities. The present system of obtaining permission to enroll in high schools and universities does not include any objective evaluation of the abilities and gifts of the students, and there is no concern for the development of their talents. What matters is, on one side, the "reward" for political "engagement" and conformity and, on the other, the punishment of parents for their political views.

These politically motivated, discriminatory actions affect the most sensitive sphere of human relations, the one between parents and children. They intimidate both the parent and the child; they enforce a formal obedience and affected attitudes; they deform the character of parents and children in the same way that certain behavior affects the fate of hostages; and they force parents and children to play a humiliating role in order to receive rewards.

While this discrimination is never openly admitted, it is emphatically enforced by the state and its political apparatus. This contradicts the claim that a socialist society offers its citizens the opportunity to develop their talents. Instead of gifted applicants, students with average or below-average grades are accepted into our schools simply because their parents either actually "engage" themselves or pretend to do so, and because they are prepared to accept and verbally support whatever the present political administration proclaims.

As proof of the existence of discrimination and favoritism, consider the official instructions from the Ministry of Education for admission in 1976–77. According to these instructions, an applicant who graduated from high school with grade 1, passed the written exam with a 1, and had an excellent oral exam, but does not meet the "class-political criteria," has to be put behind an applicant who graduated with a 2.7, whose written exam was not satisfactory, whose oral exam was average, but who fulfills the other, more crucial "criterion." These official instructions do not stimulate students in high school nor offer them the incentive to increase their knowledge and become industrious students. Just the opposite, in fact.

In addition:

1. The instructions and rules for admission are secret and not subject to public control. Lack of knowledge about these instructions gives most of the applicants no chance to prepare themselves.

2. The whole procedure for admission is secret and without any public control.

3. Not even the figures establishing the number of students to be admitted is made public. The enrollment in some disciplines is artificially reduced, especially in the non-technical areas, and the possibility of enrolling in these disciplines is still further reduced for politically unsatisfactory young people; students gifted in language, music, or the arts are at a particular disadvantage here. In this context it should be understood that according to our laws, in a number of disciplines, not only ability and concrete examples of this ability are required but also report cards (for instance, for musicians, painters, writers, translators, etc.) that reflect this ability. From the society's point of

view it should be obvious that these practices are depriving the nation of a properly educated intelligentsia in the fields of science and art.

4. Openings in certain special fields, such as art history, are kept secret. In certain cases no applications were accepted for a whole year, and it was only after the academic year had begun that children of persons "prominent" in the government were admitted.

5. In certain cases students from these "prominent" circles were admitted without examinations.

6. The chances for young people who are politically discriminated against are reduced still farther by the improper support given to less gifted students who are politically "desirable." The "politically desirable" block openings, particularly in the first semester of the year, and despite the advantages they enjoy, then later leave. Thus, a high "mortality rate" can be found, particularly in fields where examinations are strict, such as in medicine and other technical fields. There is nothing but a waste of the school's time and the state's money and, as such, a burden to all of us. At the same time it is another example of the way in which young people from other socio-political and economic categories are deprived of their right to learn and of how the general level of qualifications is lowered.

7. All of these methods degrade human values in the educational system and create "protectionism" of all kinds. People speak of bribery; this is difficult to prove. No one would admit to having "paid off" a university in order to enroll his child. The Ministry of Education should find the ways and means to confirm such activity and put a stop to it.

The demoralizing effects of the present methods of selection do harm to the moral profile of our youth. Young people learn very early the difference between eloquent declarations and the reality they hide. This affects both the unjustly discriminated against and the unjustly privileged.

Teachers, too, feel the demoralizing effects of this system, which make it difficult, if not impossible, to apply proper pedagogical methods in teaching their students. They are forced into the same moral dilemma as the parents, because if they do not act according to the established instructions, they may lose their jobs.

Apart from contributing to the undermining of moral values, pretense, and "protectionism," these practices have other consequences in both professional and practical life. The entire society is deprived of creative forces and new talent. This is particularly important and frightening to us, because our nation is very poor in raw materials and other large resources for growth. Those responsible for our greatest raw material—the creative abilities of our youth—should be aware of the great and irreplaceable loss to the whole nation.

Furthermore, the educational authorities who are responsible for the decisions concerning admission policies are ignoring the solemn international promises made by our political representatives and are thereby flagrantly violating Czechoslovak laws.

We the signatories of Charter '77 hereby request:

1. that all discriminatory instructions, rules, and policies concerning the admission of young people to our schools, insofar as they contradict the Charter of Human Rights, be abolished. This Charter is now part of the Czechoslovak legal order, and as such, we ask that Article 26 of the Charter, in particular, be respected. It states that "the law forbids any kind of discrimination and guarantees all persons the same, effective protection from any kind of discrimination for whatever reasons";

2. that public acknowledgment be made in our press that Czechoslovakia has accepted the obligation to follow paragraph 40 of the Charter, according to which the "participating government must notify the public of all measures taken to implement the rights acknowledged in this agreement";

3. that a commission consisting of teachers and administrators in the educational system who are not guilty of discriminatory practices be set up to make an objective analysis of the present situation with regard to admissions policies. They should evaluate the consequences of this critical situation for our educational potential and for our economic, technical, cultural, and moral development;

4. that after the results of this analysis by the described

commission have been considered, all students who have
been subjected to discrimination be given the opportunity to
study.

The signatories of Charter '77 feel that it would be advanta-
geous to collect concrete examples of discriminatory practices
and present them to responsible political officials, along with a
request to have them probed and to seek remedies.

The signatories of Charter '77 also regard it as their moral
and political duty to assist in the elimination of these practices
and emphasize that they have no other political aims or demands in this regard.

Finally, they see in this document the initiative for qualified action that would lead to the abolition of prevailing practices. This would allow students to be admitted to schools and
universities for the purposes of study, according to the Charter
of Human Rights, which has been accepted by the Czechoslovak government.

> The Spokesmen for Charter '77
> PROF. JAN PATOČKA
> VÁCLAV HAVEL, currently in prison
> PROF. JIŘÍ HÁJEK

CHARTER '77: DOCUMENT NO. 6*

Charter '77 is an act that falls within the right to petition and
to express one's views freely, a right guaranteed by our Constitution. Nevertheless, the co-signers of the Charter have been
exposed to numerous police actions and limitations of their
freedom, as if the writing and distribution of Charter '77 were
a punishable act. We would like to give a brief summary of the
actions taken against the co-signers and spokesmen to the extent that we have been able to ascertain them. We would also
like to request compensation for those harmed, if this is at all
possible.

*Document No. 5 contains the list of signatures reprinted in Document No. 8.

First of all, we would like to report what is already known about the signatories that have been arrested.

The writer Václav Havel has been in prison since January 14, and a week before that, he was subjected to the lawless actions of the police. On January 11 he was interrogated for an entire day in Ruzyně prison. In his absence the police photographed and searched his apartment, and later his country home in Vlčice was searched and the entire property filmed.

Neither friends nor relatives have seen Havel since the 14th of January. Consequently, he could not have his car inspected by the official technicians. (This is one of the methods the police use to harass the signers of Charter '77. They are asked to have their cars inspected by officials, and if the slightest malfunction is found, the car is taken off the road. This happened to poet Jaroslav Seifert's car because it had a few spots of rust on the body. The intent, of course, is to limit the mobility of the signatories.) On January 16 Mrs. Havel received a letter informing her that her husband had been arrested and indicted according to paragraph 98 of the Penal Code; he had requested legal counsel. The Prosecutor General's notification of the arrest was dated January 18. On January 21 Havel's typewriter was confiscated, and a new investigator appeared. On January 26 the defendant met his lawyer, Dr. Lukavec, for the first time.

As a matter of fact, Dr. Lukavec was not present at the interrogation of the witnesses, and he did not receive any written evidence against his client. He informed Mrs. Havel that her husband was in good physical condition and that the interrogation was taking the form of literary discussions. Mrs. Havel received two letters from her husband, and he received one parcel from her but not her letter. Finally, Dr. Lukavec declared that he was going to abandon the case.

At almost the same time as Havel, František Pavlíček and Jiří Lederer, the publicist, were arrested. They were accused, together with Ota Ornest (who is not a signer of Charter '77), of the crimes of attempting to overthrow the republic and acting against the interests of the republic abroad. (The connection between Ota Ornest and the others is unclear; only the media hint at some kind of tie.) The respective organs of the government have not, at this point, informed either the relatives of the accused or the public about exactly what concrete charges have been made. Meanwhile Ota Ornest is seriously ill; he had a heart attack before his arrest and is a diabetic.

These circumstances and others, particularly the silence of the state and judiciary agencies, force us to request, according to Article 29 of the Constitution of Czechoslovakia, the immediate release of Václav Havel, František Pavlíček, Jiří Lederer, and Ota Ornest. If the judicial agencies dealing with these cases find this proposal unacceptable, we ask that they make public the reasons for the arrest and persecution of these four men. If this request is not honored, it will reinforce the assumption that two citizens have been imprisoned only because they signed the Charter and another because he is one of the authors, and all this, despite the fact that the Charter is being unlawfully persecuted.

In this regard we would like to draw the attention of the nation to a whole series of repressive acts to which the signatories of the Charter have been exposed. Nearly all the signers have been called as witnesses or brought before the investigators and asked about the Charter. The authors and other signatories are interrogated repeatedly, often for the entire day. These interrogations continue, and citizens who have already made depositions are summoned again; most of them have stood upon their right to remain silent.

The State Security forces have made fifty home searches, mostly at the homes of the signatories. Printed matter, manuscripts, correspondence, and other items have been confiscated, many having no connection at all with the interrogations. Officials have taken typing samples from typewriters and, in some cases, even the typewriters themselves. Jan Patočka's manuscripts were among those taken away. According to incomplete reports, the homes of the following signers of the Charter have been searched: Milan Balabán, Rudolf Battěk, Jan Beránek, Toman Brod, Karel Čejka, Jiří Dienstbier, Bohumil Doležal, Michael Dymáček, Vratislav Effenberger, Karel Fridrich, Jiří Hájek, Václav Havel, Ladislav Hejdánek, Oldřich Kaderka, Alfréd Kocáb, Božena Komárkova, Anna Koutná, Pavel Landovský, Jiří Lederer, Ladislav Lis, Jaroslav Mezník, Milan Otáhal, František Pavlíček, Jan Petránek, Zdeněk Pokorný, Zdeněk

Přikryl, Miloš Rejchert, Aleš and Zuzana Richterovi, Jan Šabata, Ladislav Šabata, Miluše Stevichová, Jan Trefulka, Jakub Trojan, Milan Uhde, Zdeněk Urbánek, Ludvík Vaculík, Zdeněk Vokatý, Petr Zeman, Antonín Vyroubal, and Václav Vrabec. Eighteen of these are from Brno.

Some of the signers were immediately removed from official positions or dismissed from their jobs and are now concerned about how they will live. As far as we know, the justification for this action is always the appearance of the individual's name on the list of signatures of Charter '77. Officially, the employer gives the reason for dismissal as gross neglect of discipline (according to paragraph 53b of the Labor Laws) or violation of the security of the state (paragraph 53c), and sometimes the causes are completely illegal. In this way the following have been dismissed: Zdeněk Mlynář, Dr. František Jiránek, Dr. Radim Palouš, Anna Fárová, Ivan Medek, Helena Seidlová, Drahuše Proboštová, Jakub Trojan, K. Dvořák, Milan Machovec, Petr Pithart and Oldřich Hromádko. Miluša Stevichová and Jaroslav Litera were fired during their first month of probation, without any reason given. Other signers expect similar fates based on conversations they have had with their employers who have organized campaigns against them in their workshops. Jiří Ruml, Jan Sokol, and Václav Trojan lost their memberships in the trade union; Jitka Bidlarová and Zuzana Dienstbierová are no longer permitted to be members of the brigade for socialist work.

Some measures taken against the signers have had serious consequences for their health. For instance, Jelena Mašínová had a bad cartilage problem in her right leg (her doctors had recommended surgery) when she was forced to go for interrogation. Nina Kočová was made to stay in isolation in the department of venereology, although there was no reason to suspect her of being ill. From the 21st through the 24th of January the writer Karel Sidon was held by the security agents. After forty-eight hours nothing criminal had been found; he had been illegally deprived of his freedom for more than two days. On January 21 security agents used force against Josef Suk; afterward they searched his home and took typing samples from his typewriter. On January 31 Ivana Hyblerová was discharged from the company hospital in Česke Lipe "in danger of suffering a miscarriage" and declared unfit for work. Nevertheless her employer claimed that she was fit for work without any medical examination whatsoever. On that day her month-long probation period, during which an employee can be fired without justification, expired. She could now get medical attention only in Prague, sixty miles away.

On the 10th of January the mass media started a campaign against Charter '77. They have not only used defamatory statements and lies, but have also operated illegally in the private sphere and even made use of anti-Semitism. These attacks were directed primarily against Václav Havel, Pavel Kohout, Zdenék Mlynář, František Kriegel, and especially Ludvík Vaculík. This defamation of individuals still continues, and despite Article 17 of the Agreement on Citizens' and Human Rights, none of those attacked have been given the opportunity to respond to the unlawful affronts to their dignity. They have not even been permitted to present a proper interpretation of Charter '77 and to defend its theses.

Ludvík Vaculík filed suit against the official press agency, CTK, because it was distributing indecent photographs; CTK filed a countersuit against Vaculík for insult. A program of defamation and repression has been instigated against Pavel Kohout through threatening letters. The contents of these letters are intended to frighten him into thinking that he may be harmed or killed. Driver's licenses have been taken away from some signatories; others have been refused permission to use their cars. Even the driving licenses of physicians have been taken away and, in some cases, also those of their relatives. Věra Jarošová was particularly hard hit by this since she was a professional driver.

The telephones of both authors of the Charter who are still free have been disconnected, as well as those of Pavel Kohout, Erika and Miroslav Kadlec, František Kriegel, Gertruda Sekaninová-Čakrtová, Petr Uhl, Ludvík Vaculík, and František Vodsloň. Some of these people have already received notices saying that the public interest made it necessary to use the phones for other purposes.

Even the identity cards of some of the signatories have been taken away. They now have only substitute cards, which do not entitle them to take money from accounts which contain any money from abroad, nor can they use the cards for identification purposes in hotels. The state agencies have demanded that some signatories make applications to leave the country (Zdeněk Mlynář, František Kriegel, Milan Hübl, Pavel Kohout, and Ludvík Vaculík). By contrast, Evžen Menert, another signer, applied for permission to leave the country and was told by government officials that this would be a very lengthy procedure.

Security forces have summoned some signers and demanded that they withdraw their signatures from Charter '77. These demands were followed by threats or, in some cases, offers to improve their situation. Despite their lack of success in an overwhelming majority of cases, State Security is continuing this activity.

Apart from the actual signers and their families, many of those who did not wish to have their names published have been hurt. Friends of the signatories, people who cooperated with them, and other citizens who had expressed their agreement or support verbally are also subject to harassment. The elder of the Czech Evangelical Church, Václav Kejř, was interrogated in Ruzyně prison because his congregation did not condemn Charter '77 but was neutral to it. The Czechoslovak press misinformed the public by declaring that the Church had condemned the Charter.

Twenty-five workers of Suprafon (a state music concern that produces tapes, records, etc.) protested against the firing of Ivan Medek. Under pressure from the director of Suprafon, eighteen withdrew their protests. Of the seven who refused to do so, three were fired and two others harmed in different ways. The home of Dr. Alena Čapková was searched, and her typewriter confiscated, because she had transcribed Charter '77. Karel Freund had his home searched twice. The Princs, married friends of Miluše Ševichová, who lives in their house, are having serious problems maintaining their livelihood. One of the most serious cases is that of the teacher Jan Urban, who was dismissed because he refused to sign a resolution condemning Charter '77. Professor J. Košinová would not support a resolution condemning the Charter and was accused of being part of a potential back-up force of the "anti-state group" supporting the Charter.

As spokesmen for Charter '77 we regard it as our duty to publish all of these conditions. Thus, the citizens who identify themselves with Charter '77 and who express their desire to have their signatures published will have a clear picture of the possible consequences, and they can determine their relationship to it on this basis. We repeat that the Charter is not a closed society but an alliance of all who find it correct and useful to implement the two international agreements concerned with civic, political, economic, and cultural rights—agreements whose principles have become part of our system of law.

Charter '77 is open, without exception, to all Czechoslovak citizens. We appreciate the support of all adherents of human rights. The solidarity of the working population, their organizations, and the progressive forces of Czechoslovakia and elsewhere in the world will help the signers fulfill the task set down by Charter '77. As an expression of this commitment, we are proud to be able to publish the names of another 209 signers on February 1.

PROF. JAN PATOČKA
PROF. JIŘÍ HÁJEK

CHARTER '77: DOCUMENT NO. 7

Since the publication of Charter '77 we have been concerned with social and economic rights. In this document it is our purpose to summarize our views on these issues.

Both international agreements signed in Helsinki that are referred to in the Charter are guided by the ideal of freedom for all. It is also important to mention that the international workers' movement has, for a long time, been fighting to free all people from fear and need and, in fact, has formulated a radical platform supporting human rights. It has been and continues to be the goal of the socialist movement to create conditions in which workers will not be exploited. Until this goal is achieved, a simple and unconditional demand prevails, which is that those who enter the labor market should enjoy the best possible working conditions. All citizens should have not only the right to work but also the right to choose their work; all should receive wages that guarantee a decent standard of living, and should have the right to negotiate wages and working conditions as equal partners with their employers. All workers should have the right to organize trade unions. These provisions are included in the international agreements on economic, social, and cultural rights, and have become part of Czechoslovakia's code of laws.

The co-signers of Charter '77 are citizens of different political views who have in common a firm belief in the principles stated in these agreements. We have concluded that the present situation regarding economic and social rights in Czechoslovakia is of such a nature that it prompts us to offer an objective evaluation, which we will begin in this document.

1. One of the most important articles of the Helsinki Agreement is concerned with the individual's right to work and to do so in a position that he can "freely choose or accept" (Article 6). We are often confronted with the argument that this right has already been realized in Czechoslovakia, where, as opposed to capitalist countries, there is no unemployment. It is true that Czechoslovak workers are not threatened with mass unemployment and, in this respect, enjoy more security than workers in other developed countries. However, the price we have had to pay for this has been unnecessarily high.

While everyone in Czechoslovakia has the right to work, the effective output of our economy has declined and a hidden unemployment has developed. Many institutions and places of employment have been created that at this stage of technological development are obsolete. This state of affairs is compounded by the fact that workers have only limited rights in choosing their work, changing jobs, or not working at all. They are prosecuted for violating work regulations, which are becoming more strict.

At the moment the state has a monopoly on employment, the unification of the workers is being restricted, and trade unions are actually run by organs of the government.

2. The international agreements provided for fair wages, which would reflect the right of the individual to a decent standard of living for himself and for his family. In Czechoslovakia this right is an illusion. Only in the most exceptional cases are the wages paid to a worker enough to sustain his family. This is the reason so many women are employed in Czechoslovakia, which has the highest percentage of working women in the world.

Everyone knows that the government makes a virtue of necessity, and this situation is no exception. It is not true that most Czechoslovak women work in order to have a more meaningful life or more independence, but rather because their husbands' earnings are not sufficient to maintain even a half-way decent standard of living for their families. Thus, this widespread employment of women actually reflects a high degree of dependence rather than independence and is not at all an expression of their equality to men in the labor market.

Furthermore, women are discriminated against in terms of both the work available to them and the wages they receive. Infrequently published statistics show that in the 1970s women earned an average of one-third less than men, and in areas and occupations where women represent the majority of workers, wages are below average. The decision as to whether a man or a woman should be given a certain job is often arbitrary. Also, working conditions in those areas where women play an important role (the light industry, agriculture, retail stores, etc.) are far from satisfactory, and it is in these areas especially where the work is hardest.

Finally, the official organizations representing Czechoslovak women either do not complain with sufficient force or do not complain at all. Proposals for far-reaching improvements in the situation are not registered with the executive branch of the government; instead, energy is concentrated on proving that the problem of equal rights for women has already been solved. Due to legislative procedures, the creation of an organization which would represent the interests of women in this country is impossible.

3. Women are not the only group of workers who suffer discrimination; there are many others. The treatment of

younger workers differs from that of older ones; blue-collar workers are viewed differently from white-collar workers; the wages paid to the highly qualified are not much different from those paid to the unqualified, and certain branches of production receive better treatment than others.

One widespread and often recurring form of discrimination—as far as rewards for work are concerned—is the so-called "personal evaluation," which permits political considerations to take precedence over objective qualifications. This of course violates everyone's right to equal opportunity, for it introduces criteria for evaluation other than length of employment and ability. This form of discrimination becomes more obvious the more decisions (based on what is called "political involvement") disregard social needs.

This practice is particularly detrimental to the appointment of responsible supervisors in factories, and to one's chances of being promoted in certain jobs. In most cases, members of the Communist Party are the privileged workers. As a result, economic and professional management has become simply another component of the political power apparatus. This cripples the overall effectiveness of job management and supervision because it is the need to preserve the regime rather than each individual's productivity that is the basis for appointments. Under the present system the criteria for evaluating and rewarding leadership have little to do with efficiency.

4. Regarding the activities of trade unions in Czechoslovakia, we have witnessed the elimination of established practices, as well as open violations of the law. The right of trade unions to "free activities" (Article 8), "the right of all working people to organize their own unions," and "the right to choose a trade union" are all denied. Trade unions are controlled by economic organs or other branches of the government rather than by the workers themselves. Thus, the role that trade unions have played for centuries has suddenly been eliminated.

Already we have forgotten that in the years immediately following the Second World War, not only trade unions but also workers' committees were established and had great power. They actively participated in managerial affairs and played an important role in the political and socioeconomic fields. It has even been forgotten that these workers' committees were very similar to the workers' councils introduced in 1968.

In 1969 a sociological research study concerned with how workers felt about their jobs included the following statistics:

ENJOYMENT OF WORK	BEFORE AUG. 1968	AFTER AUG. 1968
much more than before	46.8%	0.9%
a little more than before	20.1%	2.6%
unchanged	21.0%	11.3%
a little less than before	4.9%	14.2%
much less than before	3.1%	68.1%
uncertain	4.2%	2.8%

The trade unions of today are no longer concerned with whether the masses of workers can participate in wage-policy decisions at either the national or local level. They openly admit that these decisions are being made solely by the leadership. When workers object to a reduction of wages (as was the case in 1972–73), the trade unions do not give them any support. If workers strike—which rarely happens, though the right to strike is "guaranteed" by the law—they are betrayed by their own unions. Trade unions do not even concern themselves with the establishment of minimum wages, leaving them to be fixed unilaterally by the government year after year.

Now, the trade unions are well-informed about working conditions and the standard of living. They have all the relevant data concerning the decline of real wages due to hidden or open increases in prices, and also know about the shortcomings in the management of housing. Nevertheless, they make no attempt to work for a solution to these problems. Instead of fighting for a share in the decision-making process, they avoid any confrontation with the establishment. As a result, they must share the responsibility for the decisions made by the government bureaucracy.

Instead of operating in the interest of the workers, and

presenting their views and concerns to the government, the trade unions participate in morale-boosting campaigns that focus, for instance, on making full use of every working hour. It is a generally known fact that Czechoslovak workers put in what may be the shortest actual working hours in Europe, and this occurs in most cases with the approval of management. However, it is also generally known that overtime and work on Saturdays and Sundays make for the longest working hours in Europe. This paradoxical situation is not an accident: It is the result of a spontaneous effort on the part of our working population to receive decent wages for its labor. The Czechoslovak worker does not expend all his energy during official working hours; he saves himself to work overtime or in the "black" labor market. (Low-commodity productivity, which creates a high demand for goods, increases the desire to work.) For the majority of workers, therefore, overtime pay is an important part of their weekly wages. Still, trade unions do not care about these important economic problems, although a number of solutions are possible. For instance, establishing a shorter work week, perhaps forty-two and a half hours or even less, while maintaining present wages (or even increasing wages in some occupations), would compensate for the increase in wages the workers are seeking.

It would be pointless to expect trade unions, which are actually nothing more than appendages of the economic apparatus, to attempt to change their roles and attitudes. We do not anticipate that they will suddenly become concerned with the workers' right to fair wages and take the necessary initiative to bring about change. However, this should not prevent any individual who is concerned with these issues to avoid taking action on his own. Every individual who feels responsible for his fellow-man should demonstrate his interest in the realization of the rights recognized by the Helsinki Agreement on Economic, Social, and Cultural Rights, and in its preamble.

Our criticism of trade unions may still be expanded. For instance, consideration could also be given to the workers' right to safe and orderly working conditions and to the problem of commuting to and from work.

These problems can be solved only through the free discussion and dissemination of ideas. To remain silent, or to state that these problems are exaggerated will only intensify the existing contradictions and aggravate the present situation. Therefore, it will be the task of Charter '77 to offer a critical analysis of Czechoslovakia's social and cultural life and to open this analysis to national discussion.

Many of the questions we have raised can be answered positively if we compare the present with the past. Yet the crux of the matter is not in comparing losses and gains in economic and social rights but in existing attitudes to these rights. We regard it as our duty as citizens to oppose the view that all working people in this country have already achieved perfect social security and that all their rights are safeguarded. In particular, we stand opposed to the belief that with the implementation of the right to work and other basic rights, all others, and especially the right to political freedom, will lose their importance.

It is a fact that our working class does not function in a capitalist market. However, it does not follow that all their rights are respected. Only the working population can be the true advocate of its own interests and civil and political rights, and when it is deprived of these rights, adverse consequences for the whole social and economic fabric must necessarily follow. We concur with the agreement on social and economic rights, and we are convinced that we can realize democratic freedom.

Finally, we would like to stress that the goal and meaning of socialism is not only to guarantee social and economic rights. Far more important is the creation of a social order in which the full and complete development of each individual can be realized—a liberation of man in the deepest and most significant sense of the word. Much would still remain to be done to achieve this goal, even if all citizens of Czechoslovakia enjoyed the economic, social, and cultural rights specified in the Helsinki Agreement.

PROF. JAN PATOČKA
PROF. JIŘÍ HÁJEK
Prague
March 8, 1977

CHARTER '77: DOCUMENT NO. 8

This is a list of 617 citizens who agree with Charter '77 and who wish to have their names published. The list is not complete, for due to various circumstances and interferences many names did not reach the spokesmen of the Charter in time to be included.

PROF. JAN PATOČKA
PROF. JIŘÍ HÁJEK

Pavel Aixner, worker
Libor Albert, worker
Jiří Aubrecht, worker

Dr. Stanislav Balák, CSc.*
Ivan Bálek, worker
Milan Balabán, priest
Zdeněk Bárta, worker
Dr. Karel Bartošek, CSc.,
  historian
Zdeněk Bartošek, worker
Jaroslav Bašta, worker
Ing. Rudolf Battěk,
  sociologist
Edmund Bauer, priest
Jan Bednář, student
Jiří Bednář, electrician
Josef Bednařík, worker
Otka Bednářová, journalist
Jindřich Belant, fitter
Jarmila Bělíková,
  psychologist
Ing. Antonín Bělohoubek,
  technician

*CSc. = Candidate of Sciences

Dr. Václav Benda,
  philosopher and
  mathematician
František Beneš, artist
Marie Benetková, housewife
Zbyněk Benýšek, artist
Dr. Jan Beránek, historian
Jitka Bidlasová, employee
Ivan Binar, teacher
Tomáš Bísek, priest
Prof. František Bláha,
  physician
Pavel Blattný, artist
Dr. Pavol Bláza,
  philosopher
Alexandr Blažik, Jr.,
  porter
Jaroslav Blažka, worker
Marie Blažková, housewife
Miloslav Boháček, worker
Jan Bok, employee
Ing. Antonie Boková,
  political scientist
Jiří Boreš
Lída Borešová, retired

Jaroslav Borský, state
employee
Antonie Botová, programmer
Zdeněk Bonaventura Bouše,
priest
Dr. Jiří Brabec, literary
historian
Vratislav Brabenec, musician
Ing. Vladimír Braha,
worker
Eva Brahová, employee
Eugen Brikcius, worker
Dr. Toman Brod, CSc.,
historian
Daniela Brodská, priest
Tomáš Brunclík, philosopher
Helena Bukovanská, artist
Ing. Jaroslav Bureš,
economist
Karel Bureš, technician
Aleš Březina, worker
Ing. Stanislav Budín,
journalist

Michal Cedrych, student
Ladislav Cerman, worker
Daniela Cíchová, employee
Vladimir Cihelka, worker
Dr. Josef Císařovský,
art critic
Victor Cohorna, retired
Milos Čečrdle, worker
Vlado Čech, programmer
Miluše Čechová, psychologist
Ing. Karel Čejka,
technician
Miroslava Černá-Filipová,
journalist
Otto Černy, worker

Prof. Václav Černý, literary
historian
Egon Čierny, historian
Dr. Stanislav Čihák,
philosopher
Dr. Jiří Čutka, scientist

Věra Daněčková, worker
Jiří Daníček, worker
Juraj Daubner, philologist
Karel Dedecius, worker
Miroslav Dedecius, worker
Ivan Dejmal, gardener
Jiří Dienstbier, journalist
Zuzana Dienstbierová,
psychologist
Václav Diviš, priest
Blanka Dobešová, librarian
Jana Dobrá, decorator
Luboš Dobrovský, journalist
Ing. Petr Dobrovský,
technician
Ing. Jindřich Dohnal,
economist
Antonín Dolejš, machinist
Bohumil Doležal, literary
critic
Dr. Jiří Doležal, CSc.,
historian
Josef Doležal, retired state
employee
Jaroslav Doucha, plumber
Růžena Drozdová, journalist
Dr. Irena Dubská,
philosopher
Dr. Ivan Dubský,
philosopher
Ivan Duchon, worker
Ladislav Dvořák, writer

Jaroslav Dvořák, technician
Vladimir Dvořák, stoker
Michael Dymáček, mathematician
Michal Dziaček, worker
Dr. Vratislav Effenberger

Jan Fábera
Jaroslav Fábera, watchmaker
Anna Fárová, art historian
Miroslav Feigel, worker
Jaroslav Fic, technician
Antonie Fischerová, retired
Miluše Fischerová, politician, retired
Miloš Fládr, sociologist
Petr Formánek, musician
Dr. Eva Formánková, editor
Zdeněk Fořt, journalist
Karel Fridrich, economist
Jiří Frodl, journalist

Milena Geussová, employee
Jan Glanc, worker
Gabriel Gössl, worker

Ing. Josef Hait, technician
Prof. Jiří Hájek, former Minister of Foreign Affairs
Dr. Miloš Hájek, CSc., historian
Jiří Hanák, journalist
Olaf Hanel, artist
Ing. Jiří Hanzelka, writer
Václav Havel, writer
Jaroslav Havlík, farm worker
Josef Havránek
Václav Hejda, state employee, retired

Zbyněk Hejda, writer
Dr. Ladislav Hejdánek, philosopher
Vilém Hejl, writer
Dr. František Helešic, CSc., scientist
Ing. Jiří Hermach, CSc., philosopher
Pavel Heřman, worker
Pavel Hlaváč, priest
Ludvík Hlaváček, art historian
Věra Hlaváčková, student
Josef Hiršal, writer
Dr. Josef Hodic, historian
Dr. Miloslava Holubová, art historian
Robert Horák, politician
Milada Horáková, employee
Emil Horčik, worker
Vladislav Horný, worker
Milan Hořínek
Ing. Milan Hošek, state employee, retired
Karel Houska, employee
Miroslav Hraban, Jr., designer
Jan Hrabina, worker
Jiřina Hrábková, journalist
Ing. Tomáš Hradílek
Ing. Dr. Oldřich Hromádko, Colonel of State Security, retired
Ing. Alena Hromádková, CSc., sociologist
Marie Hromádková, politician, retired
Karel Hruška, worker
Miloš Hruška, worker
Antonín Hudský, worker

Milan Hübl, CSc., historian
Dr. Václav Hyndrák,
  historian

František Chalupecký,
  worker
Vlasta Chramostová, actress
Petr Chudožilov, writer

Miroslav Ilek, worker
František Innemann, worker

Přemysl Janýr, worker
Rudolf Jaron, journalist
Dr. Karel Jaroš, CSc.,
  politician, retired
Dr. Oldřich Jaroš, historian
Dr. Věra Jarošová, historian
Marie Jelínková, retired
Prof. Zdeněk Jičínský,
  lawyer
Ing. Otakar Jílek, economist
Tomáš Jína, technician
Antonín Jíra, worker
Ing. Jaroslav Jíra, technician
Karel Jiráček, state
  employee, retired
Dr. František Jiránek,
  educator
Miroslav Jirounek, worker
Vera Jirousová, art historian
Jaroslav Jirů, CSc., historian
Dr. Miroslav Jodl, CSc.,
  sociologist
Dr. Josef John, lawyer
Ing. Jarmila Johnová,
  economist
Ing. Jiří Judl, technician
Libor Junek, worker
Pavel Juraček, film director

Alois Jurnik, worker
Jan Just, worker

Jaroslav Kabelka, worker
Petr Kabeš, writer
Dr. Rudolf Kabíček,
  psychologist
Dr. Oldřich Kaderka, lawyer
  and politician
Prof. Miroslav Kadlec,
  economist
Prof. Dr. Vladimír Kadlec,
  economist and politician
Dr. Erika Kadlecová, CSc.,
  sociologist
Jindra Kadlecová, librarian
Antonin Kamiš, worker
Walter Kanina, driver
Eva Kantůrkova, writer
Jan Kapek, technician
Svatopluk Karásek, priest
Olga Karlíková, painter
Jiří Kasal, worker
Jakub Kaše, employee
Prof. Vladimír Kašík,
  historian
Dr. František Kautman,
  CSc., literary historian
Ludvik Kavin, politician
Milan Kayser, worker
Marianna Kayserova,
  employee
Josef Kazík, worker
Jan Keller, priest
Marta Kellerova, housewife
Jan Kindl, worker
Mojmír Klánský, journalist
Alexandr Kliment, writer
Dr. Bohumil Klípa, CSc.,
  historian

Prof. Jaroslav Klofač,
sociologist
Dr. Vladimír Klokočka,
lawyer
Ing. Alfred Kocáb, priest
Dr. Jiří Kocourek,
psychologist
Zina Kočová-Freundová,
student
Dr. Luboš Kohout, CSc.,
political scientist
Pavel Kohout, writer
Vilma Kohsová, worker
Jiří Kolař, writer and artist
Ing. Ladislav Kolmistr,
politician, retired
Dr. Božena Komarková,
educator
Alexandr Komaško,
technician
Dr. Václav V. Komeda,
historian
Dr. Michael Konůpek,
philologist
Pavel Kopeček, writer
Petr Kopta, translator
František Korbela, priest
Jan Korbelik, nurse
Miroslav Korbelik, Jr.,
doorman
Vavřinec Korčiš, Jr., worker
Vavřinec Korčiš, Sr.,
technician
Jan Koroptvička, artist
Dr. Jiří Kořinek, economist
Vladimír Kos, employee
Pavla Kostková, employee
Dr. Karel Konstroun, literary
historian

Ing. J. Kotlas
Jaroslav Kouba, worker
Petr Kouba, painter
Jan Koudela, employee
Alena Koudelová,
employee
Anna Koutná, employee
Bohumil Koutný, employee
Karel Kovařik, politician,
retired
Václav Kozák, technician
Jan Kozlík, technician
Milan Král, worker
Ing. Miloslav Král, scientist
Alexandr Kramer, journalist
Bohumil Kratochvíl
Karel Kraus, translator
Dr. Jaroslav Krejčí, CSc.,
historian
Jaroslav Krejčí, Jr., fisherman
Ing. Petr Krejčí, scientist
Tatjana Krejčí, nurse
Dr. František Kriegel,
physician and politician
Andrej Krob, worker
Vladimír Kroul, retired
Daniel Kroupa, editor
Karel Krupa, worker
Vladislav Krupička, worker
Jan Křelina, worker
Ing. Jan Křen, historian
Jiří Křivsky, stoker
Ing. Karel Kříž, CSc.,
economist
René Kříž, worker
Jiří Kubiček, restorer
Marta Kubišová, singer
Lumir Kučera, worker
Jaroslav Kukal, electrician

Dr. Miloslav Kusý,
    philosopher
Karel Kyncl, journalist

Dr. Michael Lakatoš, CSc.,
    lawyer
Dr. Václav Lamser,
    sociologist
Pavel Landovský, actor
Ing. Karel Lánsky, journalist
Dr. Vasil Latta, lawyer
Jiří Lederer, journalist
Ing. Jan Leštinský,
    technician
Dr. Ladislav Lis, politician,
    retired
Oldřich Liška, state
    employee, retired
Jaromir Litera, politician,
    retired
Ing. Jan Litomisky,
    agronomist
Jan Lopatka, literary critic
Dr. Emil Ludvík, composer
Andrej Lukáček, priest
Klement Lukeš

Vladimír Macák, auto
    mechanic
Richard Macek, worker
Dr. Sergej Machonin, theatre
    critic and translator
Prof. Milan Machovec,
    philospher
Prof. Josef Malický,
    mathematician
Vladimír Malík, salesman
Václav Malý, worker
František Mareček, worker

Vladimir Marek, worker
Karel Marek, worker
Jiří Mareš, worker
Anna Marvanová, journalist
Jan Mařik, worker
Petr Mašek, worker
Jelena Mašinová, scriptwriter
Michal Matzenauer, worker
Jitka Matzenauerová,
    librarian
Marie Matzenauerová, priest
František Maxera, artist
Marta Mazánková, artist
Ivan Medek, music editor
Dr. Hana Mejdrová, CSc.,
    historian
Dr. Evžen Menert, CSc.,
    philosopher
Vladislav Merhaut,
    technician
Dr. Jaroslav Meznik,
    historian
Otakar Michl, programmer
Dr. Karel Michnak,
    philosopher
Stanislav Milota, cameraman
Otakar Mika, miner
Ing. Ivan Miluška,
    programmer
Dr. Ján Mlynárik, historian
Dr. Zdeněk Mlynař, CSc.,
    lawyer and politician
Ervin Motl, journalist
Kamila Moučkova, TV
    announcer
Jiří Mrázek, stoker
Petr Mudrik, worker
Jiří Müller
Vera Münzová, retired

Rudolf Münz, retired
Dr. Pavel Muraško,
    philologist
Ing. Oldřich Musil,
    technician
Jana Musilová, housewife

Dr. Jaromir Navrátil, CSc.,
    historian
Jan Nedvěd, journalist
Dana Němcová
Helena Němcová, journalist
František Němec,
    technician
Jiří Nemec, psychologist
Dr. Vladimir Nepraš,
    journalist
Vladimir Nepustil,
    psychologist
Jana Neumanová, CSc.,
    historian
Jiří Novák, stoker
Jiří K. Novák, artist
Miloš Novák, worker
Václav Novák, state
    employee, retired
Jaroslava Nováková
Radka Nováková, nurse
Zuzana Nováková,
    gardener

Bohuslav Odolán, worker
Josef Olšanský, decorator
Jiří Olt, worker
Dr. Jaroslav Opat,
    historian
Josef Opočanský, worker
Tatjana Oppelová, social
    worker

Dr. Milan Otáhal, CSc.,
    historian
Petr Ouda, stoker

Prof. Bedřich Pacák,
    physician
Dr. Ludvík Pacovsky,
    journalist
Ing. Zdeněk Pacina,
    employee
Ing. Jiřína Pacinova,
    employee
Jiří Pallas, technician
Martin Palouš, programmer
Dr. Radim Palouš, teacher
Prof. Jan Patočka,
    philosopher
Jan Patočka, Jr., worker
Jan Pavelka, worker
Dr. František Pavliček,
    writer
Ing. Blanka Pavlů, employee
Karel Pecka, writer
Anna Pechancová,
    bookkeeper
Pavel Pěkný, worker
Tomaš Pěkný, journalist
Jan Pellant, stoker
Jan Petránek, journalist
Miroslav Petříček, technician
Irena Petřinová, journalist
Dr. Karel Pichlik, historian
Dr. Zdeněk Pinc, social
    worker
Dr. Petr Pithart, lawyer
Bohdan Pivoňka, priest
Petr Podhrázký, journalist
Dana Podolská, nurse
Peter Pohl

Dr. Bohumil Pokorný,
historian
Ing. Zdeněk Pokorny,
technician
Rudolf Polaček, driver
Antonin Poljak, worker
Jiří Polma
František Polomik,
Jiří Popel, worker
Jara Popelová, psychologist
Milan Porada, worker
Anna Pospišilová, student
Martin Poš, photographer
Věnceslava Povolná,
philologist
Dr. František Povolny,
historian and sociologist
Ing. Václav Povolny,
programmer
Karel Prášek, journalist
Vladimir Prikazský, journalist
Drahuše Proboštová, editor
Petr Prokeš, film maker
Helena Prokopová, chemist
Josef Pros, worker
Jana Převratská, teacher
Dr. Zdeněk Přikryl,
politician
Dr. Tomaš Pštross,
sociologist
Vaclav Pulda, worker

Jaroslav Rada, worker
Petr Ragan, sailor
Marie Raganová, technician
Miloš Rejchrt, priest
Miroslava Rektorisová,
journalist
Aleš Richter, worker

Dr. Milan Richter, lawyer
Dr. Vladimír Richter,
politician
Zuzana Richterová,
housewife
Milan Roček, designer
Angelika Rommelová,
free-lance worker
Ing. Pavel Roubal, technician
Ing. Věra Roubalová,
technician
Jan Ruml, worker
Jiří Ruml, journalist
Ota Růžička, worker
Dr. Tomaś Růžička, CSc.,
physicist
Ing. Pavel Rybal, agronomist
Olga Rybková, midwife
Alena Rybová, housewife
Dr. Pavel Rychetský, lawyer
Vladimír Ríha, teacher
Dr. Marie Ríhová, CSc.

Ing. Naděžda Sábliková
Stanislav Sadílek, photo
journalist
Hubert Sadlo, worker
Vilém Sacher, lieutenant
general
Vojtěch Sedlaček,
programmer
Helena Seidlová, librarian
Jaroslav Seifert, national
artist
Dr. Pavel Seifert, historian
Dr. Gertruda
Sekaninová-Cakrtová
Ivo Semerád, forestry worker
Jan Schneider, worker

Miroslav Schneider,
  saleswoman
Naděžda Schulzova,
  university teacher
Karol Sidon, writer
Miroslav Skalický, worker
Eliška Skřenkova
Květa Slabá, hairdresser
Dr. Aleš Sládek, CSc.,
  teacher
Karel Slach, cameraman
Josefa Slánská
Jaroslav Slánský, worker
Ing. Rudolf Slánský,
  technician
Bohumir Slavík, salesman
Otokar Slavík, artist
Václav Slavík, political
  scientist
Antonin Slíva, teacher
Ing. Jan Smazal, state
  employee
Bohumil Smutný, driver
Ladislav Socha, employee
Jan Sokol, technician
Dr. Jan Souček, sociologist
Karel Soukup, forestry
  worker
Ing. Marie Soukupová,
  technician
Andrej Stankovič, poet
Jan Stehlík, carpenter
Ing. Josef Stehlík, politician
Dana Stehlíková, employee
Josef Steklý, artist
Vladimr Stern, state
  employee
Jana Sternová
Ing. Stibic, CSc., scientist
Jarmila Stibicová, teacher

Rudolf Straka, politician
Dr. Eva Stuchliková,
  psychologist
Dr. Čestmir Suchý, journalist
Jaroslav Suk, worker
Petra Suková, worker
Vera Suková, retired
Antonin Svárovsky, painter
Jan Svoboda, worker
Hana Svobodová
Xenie Svobodá, employee
Vojen Syrovatka, priest
Dorkas Syrovatková,
  nurse
Jan Šabata, stoker
Dr. Jarosláv Šabata,
  psychologist
Václav Šabata, artist
Anna Šabatová, journalist
Anna Šabatová, Jr., employee
Jan Šafránek, artist
Katrin Smrkovská
Jan Šafrata, technician
Ingrid Šafratová, technician
Antonin Šach, politician
Dr. František Samalik,
  lawyer
Boris Šapov, worker
Jiří Šašek
Jan Šeba, worker
Ing. Václav Šebek, architect
Ing. Jana Šebková, technician
František Šilar, theologian
Prof. Ing. Věněk Šilhán,
  CSc., economist
Dr. Libuše Šilhánová, CSc.,
  sociologist
Ivana Šimková, psychologist
Ing. Bohumil Šimon, CSc.,
  economist and politician

Marie Šimoníková, student
Jan Šimsa, priest
Dr. Jan Šindelař, CSc.,
  philosopher
Vladimir Škutina, journalist
Miroslav Šlanbera, worker
Ing. Karel Šling, economist
Vlastislav Šnajdr, surveyor
Pavel Šremer, microbiologist
Dr. Stanislav Štěrba
Miluše Števichová, worker
Marie Štolovská, retired
Vladimir Štučka, worker
Věra Štovícková, journalist
Věra Šubrtová, worker
Zdislav Šulc, journalist
Olga Šulcová, journalist
Dr. Miroslav Šumavský,
  historian
Petruška Šustrová, employee
Jaroslav Šváb, worker
Jiří Švejda, worker
Marie Švermová

Prof. Vladimir Tardy,
  psychologist and
  philosopher
Dominik Tatarka, writer
Petr Tatoun, worker
Jan Tesař, historian
Jan Thoma, worker
Josef Tokarz, worker
Františka Tokarzová,
  housewife
Alois Tomášek, retired
Dr. Julius Tomin,
  philosopher
Josef Topol, writer
Tomáš Toulec, technician
Jana Touškova

Jan Trefulka, writer
Karel Trinkewitz, artist
Ing. Jakub Trojan, priest
Václav Trojan, programmer
Jana Tůmová, saleswoman
František Tumpach,
  journalist
Jiří Tvrdoch, retired
Ing. Miroslav Tyl, technician

Dr. Milan Uhde, writer
Jiří Uher, compositor
Petr Uhl, technician
Ing. Antonín Uhlík, worker
Zdeněk Urbánek, writer and
  translator
Ladislav Uruba, politician
Ing. Richard Urx, technician
Luisa Urxová
Pavel Uxa, technician

Dr. Růžena Vacková, art
  historian
Ludvík Vaculík, writer
Zdeněk Vaculik, plumber
Jiří Vančura, historian
Olga Valešová, priest
Vlastislav Valtr
František Váneček, journalist
Dagmar Vaněčková,
  journalist
Jaroslav Vanek, locksmith
Jiří Vaněk, worker
Jan Vanik, worker
Zdeněk Vašek, worker
Dr. Zdeněk Vašiček,
  historian
Miloslav Vašina, theologian
Jan Vesecky, fitter
Jiří Vesely, worker

Stanislav Veselý, worker
Jan Velát
B. Verner, physicist
Jan Vit, journalist
Dr. Jaroslav Vitáček,
  politician
Jan Vladislav, writer
František Vlasák, worker
Stanislav Vlasák, employee
Tomáš Vlasák, worker
Václav Vlk, teacher
Vera Voců, worker
Roman Vobornik, worker
František Vodslon, politician
Josef Vohryzek, translator
Olga Vojáčková, journalist
Ivo Vojtišek, worker
Zdenek Vokatý, worker
Přemysl Vondra
  journalist
Josef Vondruška, house
  painter
Milan D. Vopálka, house
  painter
Květa Vořišková, worker
Dr. Vaclav Vrabec, journalist
  and historian
Dr. Tomaš Vrba, social
  worker

Josef Vydrář, professor
Ing. Alois Vyroubal,
  technician

Jaromir Wišok, artist
Robert Wittman, supervisor

Dr. Josef Záhora, retired
Dušan Zán, worker
Květuše Záňová, nurse
František Zavadil, philologist
Vladimir Zavadil, worker
Vačlav Zaspal, driver
Dr. Ing. Artur Zdráhal,
  teacher
Marie Zdráhalová, nurse
Dr. Jiřina Zelenková,
  physician
Petr Zeman, biologist
Rudolf Zeman, journalist
Zdeněk Zikmundovsky, state
  employee
Ing. Rudolf Zukal, CSc.,
  economist
Jindřich Zvěřina, worker
Dr. Josef Zvěřina, priest
Josef Zák, worker
Václav Zák, programmer

CHARTER '77: DOCUMENT NO. 9

> *Omnia sponte fluant,*
> *absit violentia rebus.*
> (Let everything happen freely
> and without violence.)
> J. A. COMENIUS

The recognition and implementation of human rights are becoming issues of crucial importance both nationally and internationally. The struggle for human dignity, respect for the individual and his faith, and freedom of conscience and conviction is increasing. At the same time, mankind is threatened by a wave of violence and terror. Human rights and principles upheld in important U.N. documents are being brutally trampled upon.

It is to be welcomed that some of these documents—the Helsinki Agreements—recently became part of our own body of laws. It is important that the Final Act of the Helsinki Agreement and the Agreement on the Prevention of Educational Discrimination were signed by representatives of Czechoslovakia, and that the General Declaration of Human Rights is considered throughout the world a document that inspires great spiritual and moral strength. Disrespect for human rights does not cause suffering only for individuals and groups in their own societies; it also threatens the international community as a whole. As this is increasingly realized, individuals and social institutions as well as governments will see the need to respect human rights and to work persistently toward their implementation.

Freedom of thought and of religion, together with all other liberties and rights of man, should be respected not because they are privileges but simply because without them society cannot become truly human. Everyone should be allowed to develop freely and to exercise his freedom by actively participating in the political life of his country and in its economic and cultural development.

The International Agreement on Civil and Political Rights proclaims in Article 18 the right to freedom of thought and of religion. It supports the right "to seek, receive, and impart information freely, regardless of whether it is oral or printed, or conveyed through art or any other means." All obstacles which hinder the implementation of these rights should be removed.

It is of the utmost importance that both believers and non-believers be able to express their opinions without fear of reprisals, even if these depart from the Party line. In addition to Article 25 of the aforementioned Agreement, which provides for equal opportunity employment, Article 2 of our Constitution, according to which "our society guarantees the equality of its citizens by creating equal opportunities in all walks of life," should also be respected.

Contrary to these principles is the practice of processing employment applications and complying with administrative procedures in such a way as to put pressure on people to "abandon their outmoded religious views." This is unconstitutional. Although religious denomination has been omitted from official documents for more than twenty years, it is well known that in many instances it nevertheless plays an important part in the evaluation of workers. It is necessary to ensure that believers and non-believers have equal opportunities to become teachers, professors, scientific workers, civil servants, employees in the courts and in the offices of the prosecutor, and in other institutions without having to hide their convictions. Ability and moral qualities should be the only criteria in deciding whether an individual is suited for a job.

The situation will improve if the right to freedom of expression is not restricted as, for example, in the case of believers who are only allowed passively to attend religious services. Believers should have the right to freely exercise and develop their spiritual lives, and to realize their aspirations in keeping with their traditions without outside interference. At the same time, they should be allowed to submit proposals to the government, to discuss their views publicly, and to publish them in both the religious and secular press. A

Christian or Jewish artist, teacher, scientist, philosopher, or theologian should have as much right to take part in the cultural life of his country as a person who is a loud advocate of Marxism-Leninism. Everyone who adheres to humanist, democratic, or atheistic traditions should have the opportunity to discuss his views in the mass media to the benefit of the whole society. It is against freedom of conscience, thought, and expression for certain occupations (e.g., teaching) to be entrusted only to people who swear allegiance to the ideology of the ruling political power.

The right to freedom of expression includes the right to receive ideas and inspiration, regardless of frontiers. This right is infringed upon if people are prevented from obtaining philosophical, theological, religious, or other literature from abroad, and from freely disseminating ideas, articles, essays, and other works across our national borders. It is time to stop the disastrous practice of curtailing access to undistorted information and ideas about Christianity and other religions. It is wrong for the dissemination of religious literature, including the Bible, to be considered a punishable offense and an anti-state act. (For example, it is absolutely forbidden for those in prison to read the scriptures.)

The state of religious instruction and the education of the young poses a special problem. Current practices should be brought in line with the principles upheld by both international agreements and by the Agreement on the Prevention of Educational Discrimination. Education should be made available to all, without any form of discrimination, and only the ability and talent of the applicant should be taken into consideration. In both agreements (Article 13 of the first and Article 19 of the second), the signatories promise to respect the right of parents and guardians to oversee the religious and moral education of their children. If this education takes place partly in school, it is the duty of the state to ease the pressure put on parents by school and other authorities not to send their children to religious classes; to prevent the ridiculing of children because of their faith or that of their parents; and to ensure that children will not suffer discrimination because of their beliefs. The Church and all families should be permitted to provide religious instruction in their customary way, regardless of the age of the persons being taught.

Our Constitution and both international covenants (Articles 28 and 21 of the first and Article 22 of the second) protect the right of peaceful assembly and freedom of association. In practical terms this means that the state must recognize the right of churches and religious societies to hold congresses and meetings of all kinds at which issues of common interest may be discussed and ideas freely exchanged. As a result the community will be strengthened as a whole. To this end there should also be special courses and seminars for believers, conferences of laymen and clergy, youth conventions, work parties, and trips for recreational and study purposes. Extensive contact between members of different churches should also be encouraged.

Moreover, the freedom of the Church and religious communities to seek ties with fraternal communities abroad is an inalienable part of the right of association and assembly, which provides for exchanges of students and teachers of theological colleges, and contacts between members and representatives of churches at various levels for the purposes of friendship and study. Contacts among Christians in the international community, and exchanges between various traditions and movements will have a positive influence on the life of the whole society.

Last but not least is the question of the social welfare of the clergy and their status vis-à-vis the labor law. There must be a full application of the principle explicitly stated in Law No. 218 (1949) that the clergy are employees of the Church and are authorized by it to carry out its mission. The situation will improve if the clergy are permitted to do their job without interference by state organs, which, often without grounds, refuse them permission to carry out their duties.

One must also be wary of unwarranted interference in the way entrance examinations to the theological colleges are conducted. The needs of the applicants and their interest and merit should be the only criteria used for evaluation.

This document is introduced by a quotation from an outstanding figure in cultural and intellectual history. His spirit is a living testimony to the fact that all the freedoms we demand are an integral part of our historical heritage and that their importance in the life of every individual, as well as in the whole society, has been long-standing. It would be tragic if inalienable human rights were regarded as principles that could expediently be subordinated to political or ideological aims. We continue to hope and believe that our social system has the capacity to ensure that all human rights are not only recognized but also realized through popular initiative in a spirit of trust and cooperation.

PROF. JIŘÍ HÁJEK,
Spokesman for Charter '77
Prague,
April 22, 1977

CHARTER '77: DOCUMENT NO. 10

Four months have passed since the publication of Charter '77, and while this is not a long period of time in the life of a nation, the events which have taken place provide sufficient ground to form some conclusions. The organs of State Security have made it impossible for us to deliver the text of the Charter to the government and the Federal Parliament, and their reaction to its publication has been quite different from their reaction to other petitions based on Article 29 of our Constitution. In past years there has never been a campaign of repression as ruthless as the one that has been waged against us. The aim of this campaign has been to discredit the Charter's spokesmen and signatories and to obscure the issues at hand. This campaign has been hysterical and brutal, and has pushed Czechoslovak journalism back to the fifties.

However, it has provoked an interest in the declaration itself and in the documents subsequently published. At the same time that Charter '77 gained great attention abroad, causing the regime to denounce our views and aims, its popularity spread quickly among Czechoslovaks. Hundreds of new signatures have been added to the Charter, and those who would not sign have expressed their support in other ways.

With some exceptions, state representatives have been reserved. They realize that Charter '77 is only calling for the fulfillment of obligations that the government has already made into law, and they do not want to be regarded as violators of the very laws they have passed. Thus, they have accused the signers of Charter '77 of being agents of Western imperialism and have given the police a free hand in dealing with them. While the government continues to speak of law and order, its agents have harassed the signatories of the Charter. They have broken into homes, conducted searches, ordered dismissals from jobs, tapped telephones, and confiscated driver's licenses and identity cards. Visits of Slovaks to Prague and Czechs to Bratislava have been prohibited, and those attempting such visits have been sent back with police escorts. The apartments of the spokesman Dr. Jiří Hájek and of the co-signers Dr. F. Kriegel and Dr. Z. Mlynař were under siege for weeks, and visitors were registered and interrogated. Visitors from abroad, even Communists, were prohibited from seeing them, and some of them were forced to leave the country. A modest estimate of the cost of this police surveillance is 350,000 kopecs.

A second spokesman for the Charter and a signatory, J. Lederer, have been imprisoned for almost four months without a court order. There are signs that a trial is in preparation. It may be that the indictment will refer to other accusations, but, in reality, it will be a trial against Charter '77. If this is not enough, the events connected with the tragic death of the spokesman Prof. Dr. Jan Patočka and his funeral are proof that certain organs of the power apparatus in this country are acting in violation of the law and without respect for human dignity.

The press campaign against the Charter, although not based on any concrete evidence, did publicize the kinds of problems that need to be solved in Czechoslovakia, and attention was focused on the issues of civil rights and democratic freedom. Thus, Charter '77 encouraged a number of citizens to make a commitment to human rights, and because of official condemnation of the Charter, the population was politicized. Some citizens, particularly people working in the arts, have been promised permission to work in their chosen field if they consent to sign a document denouncing Charter '77. All of us must decide for ourselves whether the price we are asked to pay is worth the reward we are being offered.

The government has made some superficial changes to avoid being accused of having violated Czechoslovak laws and international agreements. Changes have been introduced in high school admissions procedures, but their effects cannot yet be evaluated. Similarly, it has been reported abroad that the sale of foreign magazines and newspapers is allowed, but that is not yet a reality in Czechoslovakia.

Of great importance was the April 5th session of the Federal Parliament, which demonstrated a growing concern for and interest in human rights. Many citizens saw the convening of this session as a partial response to the declarations made in the Charter. No baseless accusations against it were to be found in either the transcript of speeches or in official excerpts of the debates. But on the contrary, the Parliament did consider, although in broad terms, the necessity of encouraging civic initiative. Unfortunately, no conclusions were drawn from the Charter's report of incidents violating the rights set forth in our Constitution and in international agreements.

The mass media could not afford to ignore the widespread discussion of the issues raised by the publication of Charter '77. Interrogations conducted by the organs of State Security leveled the most absurd accusations against Charter members and tried to link Charter '77 with imperialist and anti-Communist groups. There is little difference between these accusations and those made during the fifties, which relied on the government's monopoly of the mass media rather than on the facts to misinform the public at home and abroad.

In spite of the widespread publicity given to these accusations by the press in Warsaw Pact countries, we are pleased by the solidarity and moral support expressed by many people there, as well as by the good will of representatives of the civil rights movements that exist in these countries under difficult conditions. We are also encouraged by the solidarity expressed by Communist and socialist democrats all over the world. Their concern is the same as that of Charter '77: to respect civil and human rights as a precondition for peaceful coexistence between all countries regardless of particular ideologies or stages of development. This concern is clearly stated in the Charter of the United Nations, the General Declaration on Human Rights by the U.N., and the Final Act of the Helsinki Agreement. The reaction of the rest of the world, be it positive or negative, reflects the state of international relationships today.

Despite the anti-Charter campaigns, our tasks will continue to be to develop further the initiative of the citizenry to achieve the goals set forth in the Charter. We are convinced that certain misunderstandings concerning human and civil rights can be eliminated only in a rational and constitutional way:

a. by an objective examination of all the facts cited in Charter '77;

b. by a responsible analysis of their causes and effects;

c. by gradually abolishing that system of laws which contradicts the two international agreements and Czechoslovakia's obligation to abide by them, and by codifying the laws in such a way as to eliminate the possibility of any ambiguous interpretations.

We therefore propose:

1. that the unworthy campaign against Charter '77 be ended, and that all lawless measures applied to it and its supporters be revoked; that the costly police activities that provoke new conflicts be stopped; and that all citizens imprisoned in connection with the Charter be released immediately;

2. that the two international agreements be distributed widely enough to meet the demand; that the contradictions between the wording and the implementation of these ideas concerning human rights be made public;

3. that the decision by the Federal Parliament during the April 5th session to enforce the laws that guarantee human rights and civil freedom, and to offer recommendations and answer complaints be respected; that each citizen be given a real opportunity to register with the government complaints concerning the violation of their human rights, and that all attempts to limit such opportunities be discontinued. As the most powerful political body in the country, the Federal Parliament should deal directly with those violations that discredit

the state's policy, and force subordinate government organs to correct any wrongdoing;

4. that civil and labor laws, and the Penal Code especially, be amended, so as to bring the Czechoslovak legal system into closer alignment with the principles set forth in both international agreements. This would lead to a greater feeling of security for the general population, and to the realization of socialist principles;

5. that discussions of the recommendations and complaints made by the spokesmen for Charter '77 be allowed, as well as those made by its co-signers and any other citizens; that the present practice of allowing citizens to make complaints only in the front rooms of interrogation offices be discontinued;

6. that the Committee for Human Rights be given official recognition according to paragraph 41 of the General Declaration on Human Rights; and that this committee be notified when one of the state organs does not fulfill its obligation. If the Czechoslovak government were to accept such an international committee, its prestige in the world would be increased and the fear that its acceptance of the international agreements is only verbal and not actual, would be removed;

7. that employees of the mass media and of the security forces who abuse their positions by slandering, threatening, and pressuring our citizens be censured; that those employees be held responsible for having misused their positions in order to do harm to those citizens who have demonstrated their agreement with our Constitution and our laws. Those who have violated the laws and have failed to meet obligations stemming from the international agreements do great harm to the state's reputation. For them, a real socialist democracy is a nightmare; and, therefore, they are the most militant enemies of civil and human rights and democratic freedom. At present, they merely pose a threat by trying to revive the atmosphere of the show trials of the fifties. The political leadership has resisted their attempts, but given the opportunity and the power to do so, these people would repeat those crimes.

During the past four months Charter '77 has been subjected to careful scrutiny, and all of its points have been proven correct. Despite the pressure exerted on all its members, only one person has withdrawn his signature from the Charter, and his has been replaced by hundreds of others. Charter '77 has also maintained its legal footing: No one has been indicted because of the Charter. In addition, the fact that Charter '77 has maintained its moral character is of primary importance: The Charter and its supporters have refused to compromise their position under pressure and, at the same time, have demonstrated a willingness to cooperate with all those who wish to see human rights and the freedom of our citizens respected. In our opinion this is a most important contribution to the easing of tensions in Europe and to the development of a real socialist society in Czechoslovakia.

PROF. JIŘÍ HÁJEK
Prague
April 29, 1977

What Can Charter '77 Hope to Accomplish?

For those concerned with the future of our movement, the above question is of crucial importance. The sympathy we have won for our cause has been great; we certainly could not have expected more. But the Charter is making some people uneasy because it is always disconcerting to challenge a seemingly omnipotent regime, especially if one feels that one is walking a fragile tightrope over a bottomless abyss and is armed with only dreams and ideals. This being the case, what can Charter '77 hope to accomplish? What is its future?

Some have speculated that the Charter will succeed only in bringing about a situation worse than presently exists, and that it will force the government to silence even those not previously counted among its critics. In response I can say only this: yielding to power has never freed anyone from oppression. The more fearful and submissive the oppressed become, the greater the arrogance that the powerful assume. No, we free ourselves only by constantly reminding the regime of the injustices that we suffer. Let no one misinterpret this as an idle threat; it is an appeal to the citizenry to come forth and make themselves heard, regardless of any inconvenience they may suffer. Mass action alone will be effective

It is possible that repression will come to bear more heavily on some than on others. Many may lose their jobs, but this situation will not last forever. And nothing the leadership can do to us will make up for the loss of confidence that they will suffer. Never again will they be able to take us for granted and assume that those who obey them today will obey them tomorrow.

Now our detractors have waged a shameful campaign to vilify Charter '77. They began with impassioned polemics that were completely out of touch with the truth. They slandered us even before we had a chance to state our views, attempting to destroy the movement with lies. All of this has resulted in more support for our cause, both at home and abroad, than we ever imagined. And so the Charter has taught us at least one important lesson: forthrightness and honesty are important values in the political realm.

The fact that Charter '77 seeks only compliance with the law has been to our great advantage. As a result, those in power have been forced to think of repressive tactics other than brute force, shaky fabrications about anti-state conspiracies, and obstinate refusals to discuss the issues with those who have allegedly compromised their socialist stance. The regime should surely realize by now that not apostates but grave social ills plague Czechoslovakia.

As supporters of Charter '77, we must intensify our campaign. For how long can we count on the support of our countrymen if we continue to protest only on paper? And how long will the support of Western nations last? When will their concern for human rights give way to such issues as disarmament and trade?

We know that the struggle for human rights will not be easy as we first thought. There is both a "democratic" and a "despotic" interpretation of socialism. The latter does not promote freedom of expression, and its adherents will have a difficult time adjusting to democratic values. Some are already doing their best, but still they have much to learn.

Since the 1950s the nations of the Eastern bloc have been taking slow but sure steps to realize human rights. And so we need not be frightened by the apparent novelty of our endeavors. Let us nurture once again the feeling that there are values worth suffering for—values that make life worth living. Incidentally, these are also the values that give meaning to art and culture. Thus Charter '77 has given us a breath of fresh air.

Perhaps the leaders of the world will soon choose a new course and make policy that complies with the Helsinki accords. This would at least be a partial victory in the struggle for human rights; all nations would profit thereby. Let us see to it that this becomes a reality.

The purpose of Charter '77 has been to educate the citizenry. All of us must make ourselves aware of the important issues of our times. For this we must keep an open mind and not be driven by fear and the profit motive. We hope that Charter '77 will continue to instruct our countrymen and help them act dutifully, independently and voluntarily. We also hope that the leadership will recognize the importance of being accountable to a constituency that does not live in fear.

PROFESSOR JAN PATOČKA
Prague
March 8, 1977

Editor's Afterword

This collection of documents does not pretend in any way to be exhaustive. It was inspired by curiosity and political unease. Concerned about the scattered and incomplete reports on recent developments in Czechoslovakia, I wanted to add more information to what was already available. The documents in this volume are arranged chronologically to give the reader a sense of the continuity of events. For some time now I have been troubled by the fact that the Western media seems to exploit the political situation in Czechoslovakia to promote the ideology of the West. And so, many citizens of Eastern Europe who have been critical of totalitarianism have had to defend themselves against the misrepresentation of their views. Through this volume I hope to give them a chance to speak for themselves.

In editing this book I was guided by two principles: arranging the documents chronologically and grouping them according to whom they were addressed. It would have been possible to organize them according to their content and their relation to specific events, but this would have required copious commentaries, and I was concerned primarily with offering as many documents as possible to the reader.

Furthermore, time and certain technicalities forced me to end the book with Document No. 10 of Charter '77. It should be clear, however, that the movement for human rights in

Czechoslovakia continues at full force, though its ultimate achievement cannot be predicted.

Finally, I would like to thank everyone who has helped me in this undertaking. First, my thanks to those who translated these documents from the Czech: Mrs. Ingrid Loffler, Mr. Bedrich Utitz and Mr. Adolf Muller. Special thanks go to Ota Filip and to Adolf Muller for their assistance in recovering the letters and documents from various archives. One researcher would not have been equal to the task.

To avoid misunderstanding, I must add that most of these documents are available, in one form or another, in the West. None was written expressly for this publication and none was smuggled from Czechoslovakia. The documents of Charter '77 have been published by international press agencies. I would also like to thank Europaische Verlagsanstalt and the German and International P.E.N. for their support, as well as Arthur Miller, who wrote the foreword.

HANS-PETER RIESE

Biographical Notes*

BILAK, Vasil (b. 1917): Member of Parliament since 1945.
1950–59: functionary in the Slovak Communist Party; 1960–
62: Commissioner of Education in Slovakia; 1962: member of
the Slovak Central Committee; 1968: member of the Praesidium of the Communist Party of Czechoslovakia; January–
September 1968: First Secretary of the Slovak Communist
Party; September 1968– : Secretary of the Central Committee of the Communist Party of Czechoslovakia. A prominent
member of the pro-Soviet faction in the Party leadership of
1968.

DUBČEK, Alexander (b. 1921): 1949–60: Served in various capaci-
ties as a member of the Party in Slovakia; 1958– : member of the
Slovak Central Committee and of the Central Committee of the
Communist Party of Czechoslovakia; 1960–1963: Secretary of
the Central Committee in Prague; 1960– : member of Parliament; 1962: candidate and later full member of the Praesidium
of the Central Committee of the Communist Party of Czechoslovakia; 1963–January 1968: First Secretary of the Slovak Communist Party; First Secretary of the Communist Party of Czechoslovakia; President of the Federal Parliament in April 1969, and
ambassador to Turkey in the fall of that year; 1970: expelled

*These notes are taken from *Reform Communism and the History of the Com-
munist Party of Czechoslovakia* by Zbyněk Hejda (Europaische Verlagsanstalt,
Köln-Frankfurt, 1976)—the editor

from the Party. Dubček now lives in Bratislava and is employed by the Forestry Department.

HAJEK, Jiri (b. 1913): Functionary in the Social Democratic Youth Movement in the late 1930s; 1939–45: imprisoned by the Nazis; 1945–48: functionary in the Social Democratic Party and member of Parliament; 1948: member of the Central Committee of the Communist Party of Czechoslovakia; 1949–54: professor of economics and political science at Charles University; 1955–65: diplomatic service in Great Britain and in the United Nations; 1965–69: Minister of Foreign Affairs; 1969: member of the Academy of Sciences; 1970: expelled from the Party. Hajek is now retired and lives near Prague; he is one of the three spokesmen for Charter '77.

HAVEL, Václav (b. 1936): A prominent Czech writer. He studied at the technical university in Prague after serving in the military, and was a stagehand for the Theatre on the Balustrade. Later he served as lighting assistant, secretary, and assistant lecturer, then as dramatic producer, and as author-in-residence. As a non-Party member he delivered an important speech at the IVth Congress of Writers. A member of "Tvar" and a spokesman for the Organization of non-Party Writers, Havel was banned in 1969, and in 1977 became a spokesman for Charter '77. On January 14, 1977, he was arrested and accused of "activities hostile to the government."

HUSÁK, Gustáv (b. 1913): As an attorney in Bratislava, Husák was a member of the illegal leadership of the Slovak Communist Party in 1943 and was Commissioner of Internal Affairs during the Slovak upheaval; 1945–46: Commissioner of Transportation and Technology; 1946–50: Chairman of the Board of Commissioners; 1949–50: member of the Central Committee of the Communist Party of Czechoslovakia. Husák was arrested in 1951 and sentenced to life imprisonment in 1954; he was released in 1960 and rehabilitated in 1963. 1963–68: member of the Academy of Sciences; 1968: Deputy Prime Minister of Czechoslovakia; September 1968: First Secretary of the Slovak Communist Party and member of the Central Committee and of the Praesidium. A member of Parliament since 1969, Husák was appointed First Secretary of the Communist Party of Czechoslovakia in April of that year, and later became Secretary General. He has been President of the Republic since 1975.

HÜBL, Milan (b. 1927): 1950–64: Student, teacher, and worker at the Political University of the Central Committee of the Communist Party of Czechoslovakia; 1964–68: affiliated with the Party Institute of History; 1968–69: rector of the Political University and member of Parliament and of the National Council; 1969: ousted from all posts. Hübl was expelled from the Party in 1970 and arrested and sentenced to 6 years in prison for "hostile activities" in 1972. Released on parole, he is a signatory of Charter '77.

JANOUCH, František (b. 1931): A member of the Communist Party since 1947, Janouch studied at the University of Leningrad from 1949 to 1954 and at the University of Moscow from 1956 to 1959; 1956–57: Chairman of the Party Organization of Czechoslovak students in Moscow. In 1967 he taught at Charles University and served as head of the Department of Theoretical Nuclear Physics at the Academy of Sciences; 1967–69: chairman of the Party organization at the Nuclear Research Institute. Expelled from the Party in 1970, he was unemployed from 1970 to 1974. Along with Vaculík and Silham, he was prosecuted for giving an interview to the BBC in 1973. In 1974, he left Czechoslovakia for Sweden where he served as visiting professor at the Swedish Academy of Sciences. He has also taught in Denmark. Janouch was deprived of his Czechoslovak citizenship in 1975.

KAPLAN, Karel (b. 1928): 1956–60: Studied history at Charles University; 1960–64: political activist; 1964–70: worked at the Academy of Sciences; 1968–69: a member of the Piller Team appointed to investigate the show trials and a delegate to the IVth Party Congress. A co-opted member of the Control Commission of the Central Committee of the Communist Party of Czechoslovakia after Dubček's return from Moscow, he was expelled from the Party in 1969, and ousted from his teaching position at the Academy of Sciences in 1970. Employed as a stoker since 1970, he was arrested in 1973 but released after three months, though he is still subject to prosecution. Kaplan went into exile in 1976 and now lives in Munich.

KOHOUT, Pavel (b. 1912): As a student of philosophy at Charles University, he was editor in chief of the satirical paper *Diko-braz*, and was later an editor on various magazines and newspapers, a television reporter, freelance writer, playwright and publicist; 1949–50: cultural attaché with the Czechoslovak embassy in Moscow. In 1967 Kohout provoked an open conflict with the Party leadership by reading Alexander Solzhenitsyn's "Open Letter to the Soviet Congress of Writers" at the IVth Congress of Writers, and was expelled from the Party. Rehabilitated in 1968, he was again expelled in 1969 and banned. Kohout is a signatory of Charter '77.

KOSÍK, Karel (b. 1926): 1954–55: Editor of the philosophy journal *Filozoficky Casopis*. In 1956 he served as deputy director of the Institute of Philosophy of the Academy of Sciences, and later as professor of philosophy at Charles University; 1968–69: member of the Central Committee of the Communist Party of Czechoslovakia; 1970: removed from office and expelled from the Party.

KRIEGEL, Frantisek (b. 1908): 1936–39: Served as military physician attached to the International Brigade in the Spanish Civil War; 1940–45: military physician in the Chinese Army; 1945–49: employed by the Party apparatus in Prague; 1945–53: Deputy Minister of Health; 1953–60: worker at the Institute of Rheumatology; 1960–63: advisor on health problems to the Cuban government; 1964: deputy member of Parliament; 1966: member of the Central Committee of the Communist Party of Czechoslovakia; 1968; member of the Praesidium of the Party and Chairman of the National Front in 1968. After the Soviet occupation, Kriegel was removed from all his posts. He refused to sign the so-called "Moscow Dictate," was expelled from the Party in 1969 and retired. Kriegel is a signatory of Charter '77.

MLYNÁŘ, Zdeněk (b. 1930): 1955–56: Employed by the Prosecutor General; 1958–63: secretary of the Institute for Legal and State Affairs of the Academy of Sciences; 1964–68: Secretary of the Committee on Law of the Central Committee of the Communist Party of Czechoslovakia; 1968: Secretary of the Central

Committee. Mlynář resigned from this position in November 1968 and worked at the National Museum. Expelled from the Party in 1970, he was unemployed for years. Mlynář is a signatory of Charter '77 and recently left Czechoslovakia for Austria.

PATOČKA, Jan (1907–1977): A philosopher, he began his studies in 1926 and pursued them in Prague, Berlin, Freiburg, Paris and elsewhere. His most influential teacher was the phenomenologist, Edmund Husserl. Patočka is widely regarded as the most important translator of Hegel; 1929–39: professor of philosophy at Charles University and member of the Prague Circle; 1936: with Landgrebe he edited Husserl's posthumous writings; 1939–45: taught at Charles University and worked as a translator, chiefly of Commenius, in one of the libraries of the Academy of Sciences. After the Communist takeover in 1948, he was ousted from his teaching post because he was not a Communist. In 1963 Patočka returned to the Institute of Philosophy of the Academy of Science, and regained his professorship at Charles University in 1968. He was again dismissed from his teaching post in 1970 and forced to retire, although he continued to lecture around Prague. In 1973 he received a honorary doctorate from the University of Aachen in Germany but was not granted permission to travel abroad to receive his award; 1975–1977: elected one of the three spokesmen for Charter '77 and was interrogated by the Ministry of the Interior; March 13, 1977: Patočka suffered a brain stroke and died after long hours of questioning about his meeting with van der Stoel, Dutch Minister of Foreign Affairs.

PREČAN, Vilém (b. 1933): Precan was graduated from Charles University in 1957 and worked at the Institute of History of the Academy of Sciences until 1970, when he was fired and banned. Precan now lives in West Germany.

VACULÍK, Ludvík (b. 1926): A writer, Vaculík was expelled from the Party in 1967 for statements made at the IVth Congress of Writers. Rehabilitated in 1968, he became a member of the Central Committee of the Union of Writers, and, in June of that year, wrote his "2,000-Word Manifesto." He was expelled again from the Party in the fall of 1968 and has since been banned. Vaculík is a signatory of Charter '77.